SEEING RED

SEEING RED

THE CHIC CHARNLEY STORY

CHIC CHARNLEY

WITH ALEX GORDON

BLACK & WHITE PUBLISHING

First published 2009
by Black & White Publishing Ltd
29 Ocean Drive, Edinburgh EH6 6JL

1 3 5 7 9 10 8 6 4 2   09 10 11 12

ISBN: 978 1 84502 270 9

Typeset by Ellipsis Books Limited, Glasgow
Printed and bound by MPG Books Ltd, Bodmin, Cornwall

CONTENTS

SEEING RED

DEDICATION

Ma,

You mean everything to me. You worked your fingers to the bone for all seven of us and we never went without. I don't know how you did it. You are something else. You are always there for everyone and you mean the world to me. God bless. I love you, Ma.

James

ACKNOWLEDGEMENTS

This is for Margaret, Gary and Danielle – I don't know how they have put up with me all these years.

Also, for my granny Agnes who was such a pleasure to be with. I think of her every day.

Jimmy Pelosi, for everything he has done for my Ma over the years.

My Uncle Tommy was special to me, too, and he is always in my thoughts.

I would like to thank my former Partick Thistle gaffer John Lambie for everything he did for me in my career. He was always there for me.

Alex Gordon, my co-author, deserves a special mention, too. While doing this book we have built up a great friendship and I hope we will remain pals forever.

FOREWORD
BY JOHN LAMBIE

Chic Charnley is like a son to me. Having said that, there were times when I would quite happily have throttled him! Aye, it would be fair to say the lad possessed the ability to test the patience of a saint. And, by the way, as anyone who knows me will inform you, I am no saint.

Of course, I signed Chic on more than a few occasions. There was an excellent reason for that – Chic could play. I thought, in his prime, he was a fabulous talent, a gem of a footballer. He had vision and a breathtaking range of passing ability to make the most of it. His seventy-yard passes were a joy to behold and he can take this as a compliment, but he did it so often and was so consistent in hitting the target that no-one even passed comment. We expected a ball from Chic to lock onto his team-mate and, more often than not, that's exactly what happened.

Naturally enough, we didn't always see eye-to-eye and some words were said during rather heated exchanges during our days at Partick Thistle and Hamilton Accies. But, thank God, we have remained friends to this day and I am more than grateful for that. I've often heard people talk about Chic and I feel like screaming. There is a preconceived notion about him and so many folk just do not know the real Chic Charnley. He is one of the biggest characters in the game and has a reputation that goes with it. Some of it is extremely colourful, but, believe me, a lot of it is nonsense. I had my run-ins with him, but nothing that couldn't be resolved. We could have a good clear-the-air chat – for the want of a better description – and that would be the end of it. There was never any simmering resentment between either of us.

I know some managers who just couldn't handle Chic or his personality. I could and the reason was simple. I treated him the way he deserved to be treated – like a man. I have found that Chic would always give you respect if you didn't treat him like a kid. So, from that angle there was never a problem. As I've said, we did have our ups and downs, but never anything that soured our relationship. I have often been accused of seeing Chic as my blue-eyed boy. I'm sure he will put you right on that score elsewhere in this book.

His record of red cards doesn't tell you half the story. It's so unjust for folk to dismiss him purely as a hot-head with a bad temper. These are not football people; these are not people who understand the game. Aye, the boy had a temper and he could blow up sometimes. However, in the main, I will remember his outstanding talent and the fact that he smiled a lot. He could cry too, and that may surprise more than a few. Chic is a genuine human being with a big heart. He probably won't thank me for this revelation, but he does an incredible amount of good work for charity, most notably for Yorkhill Sick Children's Hospital in Glasgow. It's something that Chic wouldn't attract attention to or shout from the rooftops, but he gives up a lot of his spare time for these kids. Doesn't quite sit with the idea or the image some folk have of Chic, does it?

I can also recall that Thistle physiotherapist John Hart, sadly no longer with us, but, take my word for it, one of the best in the business, would fine latecomers at Firhill. He never took money off the players, but would send them out to buy Mars Bars, Bounties, Twixes and the like. When it got near Christmas

John would have a sackful of an assortment of confectionary. We never had to look too far for someone to volunteer to take the chocolates around the hospitals. Chic was always first up and he would go on his way around the wards of various hospitals distributing the goodies to unfortunate kids. It was a typical gesture from the man and underlined what I already knew about him – he was a caring, sharing kind of guy.

Chic's got time for everyone. He is one of the most approachable blokes you will ever meet and he will have a chat with anyone. He has never been Billy Big-Time and that's also to his credit. There are too many footballers around who are legends in their own lunchtime. Chic was never like that. I would see him collecting spare tickets before games at Firhill and then going out half-an-hour or so before the kick-off and giving them to kids or old-age pensioners. It was a typical gesture from the man. I swear I have seen Chic chatting with Rangers fans and signing autographs for them outside Ibrox. He was a well-known Celtic supporter, but you could never call him a bigot. No way. He was brought up a Celtic fan and he never disguised it. However, being a thorough professional, he always gave his best when we played them. I would have expected no less.

There is another thing that struck me about Chic when our relationship started all those years ago – his honesty. He never tried to bullshit you. He never offered up lame cock-and-bull excuses for missing training or being late for a session. If he was out the night before having a bevvy that went over the score and hindered him somewhat the following day, then that's what he told you. He didn't come up with any of the 'I felt the sniffles coming on, gaffer' or 'I had a dodgy stomach'. He told you straight and I actually admired him for that. I wanted to take him by the scruff of the neck and bash his head off a wall at the same time, but that would only have damaged the wall! In many ways, Chic was a man's man and I liked that, too.

As far as his sendings-off go, I never thought Chic ever got the benefit of the doubt. His reputation went before him and some referees looked as though they could not wait to banish him just to get a so-called troublemaker off the pitch. Chic suffered for that, no doubt about it. Football is an emotional game and Chic was most certainly an emotional individual. On matchday he was a highly-charged guy who couldn't wait to get out there and get in amongst it. Some match officials understood where he was coming from, but, unfortunately, there were too many who didn't. In my day you could swear at referees and they didn't take a blind bit of notice. Tiny Wharton was a top ref in his day and I called him all sorts of names, but he would merely retort, 'That's enough of that, Mr Lambie – let's get on with the game.' If Chic said something out of turn you could see the match official reaching for a yellow or red card with indecent haste. It was a real shame.

Brian McGinlay was a referee who was around for a fair bit of the time Chic was playing and I don't think he even booked him once. He knew the game and would take into account that Chic had blurted out something in the heat of the moment. He knew it would pass – as it always did. Chic might have had me pulling my hair out in clumps sometimes when he went AWOL from training – not too often, I'm glad to say – but he was a real professional on matchday. His passion and fervour for the game were obvious to everyone, whether it was in the dressing room or out on the park. He always wanted to be a winner. There were days when I was ready to kick in the dressing room door at half-time after a particularly poor display from my team. However, by the time I got there I could hear Chic and the likes of Jim Duffy doing my work for me. They would be laying into everyone and I didn't have to say a word on some occasions. I couldn't have put some of their criticisms and observations better myself. I guess I was just lucky to have such guys around.

Don't get the impression that Chic always blamed others and didn't point the finger at himself. That's way off beam. Chic was his own biggest critic. He was always quick to put up his hands and take his dumps when they were deserved. Unlike some individuals I could name and shame, Chic never hid in a game even when he was having a stinker. That always impressed me. He could be having one of those days when barely anything would go right, but he was still willing to run himself into the ground, looking to take passes and try to make things happen. You never got anything less than 100 per cent on matchday. That was when he was focused; that's where he did his work. But, as I have said, he had a temper.

I was on the receiving end of it one day when Gerry Collins was sacked as manager of Partick Thistle and Bobby McCulley, his assistant, was also handed his P45. Chic was a coach at the time and I know he loved working with Gerry and Bobby. He quit on the spot, despite being told his job was safe. However, he got it into his head that I was somehow to blame for the sackings. I don't know where that came from. Someone must have planted a seed in Chic's head and he came looking for me. 'You bastard,' he shouted. 'You bastard.' For about five minutes those words seemed to be the only two in the English language Chic knew as he kept up his tirade. I thought it was best to try and talk sense into him when he had calmed down. What Chic hadn't realised was that I had done everything in my power to keep Gerry and Bobby in their jobs. I told anyone willing to listen that they should be allowed time to turn things around. Most of my words must have fallen on deaf ears because, of course, the pair were shown the door.

Chic and I were on course for a spectacular fall-out, but, thankfully, sanity was restored and we had a good, open discussion. Eventually, it was proved that I had nothing whatsoever to do with the dismissals of two excellent professionals. Chic apologised and, as ever, that was the matter laid to rest. It didn't interfere with our friendship. Someone had done their best to stir it up between us, but had failed miserably. There are a lot of half-wits and jealous blokes in football. I've come across more than a few, I can tell you.

As everyone knows, Chic is a massive Celtic fan and I wonder what went wrong that he never signed for his boyhood favourites. I've got a fair idea. It was yours truly who gave Chic the permission to turn out for Celtic against Manchester United in the Testimonial Match for Mark Hughes at Old Trafford in 1994. He was a Partick Thistle player at the time, of course, but there was no way I would have stood in the way of him getting to play in his beloved green-and-white hoops. He was realising a dream that evening. I have been reliably informed by people whose opinion I respect that Chic was easily the Man of the Match in that encounter. I wish I had been there to see it. Chic, I'm told, was majestic, hitting killer passes all over the place with even the United fans applauding him. To make the night even sweeter, Celtic won 3-1. Lou Macari was the Celtic manager at the time and surely he must have been impressed with what he had just witnessed.

Thistle wouldn't have been difficult to deal with if Celtic had made a move for Chic, I can assure you of that. That call never came from Parkhead. Why? I can only assume that someone put the mix in for Chic. Someone must have told Celtic that he was a wrong 'un. There had been a lot said about his colourful past and a lot of it was rubbish. However, there must have been a person at Celtic who was only too willing to listen to 'advice' and not follow up their interest. If they had put a call in to me to check out Chic I would have put them straight. No-one knew him better than me, after all. I would have given an honest assessment and I'm sure that would have been enough for Chic to swap Partick for Paradise. It's a terrible pity that it never happened. If I recall properly, Thistle beat Celtic 3-1 in a league game at Hampden the following season. Those were the days when Celtic were playing at the national stadium while Parkhead was being renovated. Chic was simply wonderful that evening and had picked the perfect stage upon which to display his full range of passing. I thought he was outstanding too, as Celtic were taken apart. It was as though he had something to prove. Of course, he didn't. We all knew about his qualities and he had demonstrated them on a consistent basis over many years. However, he could have so easily been playing against Thistle that night and it would have been us on the receiving end.

Chic's footballing ability could never be questioned. I also remember working on a tactic in training that we were going to put into use in a game against Rangers. I was looking for us to do something right from the kick-off, but for my idea to work then we had to have someone who could pass the ball with laser-beam precision. Step forward, Chic Charnley. Luckily enough, we did win the toss and elected to kick-off. There were two touches before it arrived at Chic's trusty left foot and he sent a sizzling through pass into the tracks of John Flood and – bang! – the ball was in the Rangers net. It had all happened in the space of seconds, but it could only have borne fruit if you had a guy like Chic in your team.

Chic took some stick every time he played against the Ibrox lads. He loved to wind them up and they barracked him mercilessly. I don't think they even booed and jeered Celtic players as much as they targeted Chic. On the face of it, he could take it. He gave the impression he was even thriving on it. Deep down, though, I realised it might just get to him. But that's Chic. A lot of people just don't have an inkling about what makes him tick. Will the real Chic Charnley please stand up? Everyone I know who meets Chic for the first time doesn't know what to expect from him. They've heard all the daft stories, of course.

They think they might be meeting a cross between Al Capone and Adolf Hitler. As they soon find out, nothing could be further from the truth. Chic smiles a lot and, in the main, has a sunny disposition. I wouldn't have spent so much time with him if it was the reverse, trust me on that. I still like his company and I have always found him to be extremely knowledgeable about football and that, too, may surprise a few out there. He has opinions, as well, and he is not afraid to air them.

I go to a lot of games with my former Thistle chairman Jim Oliver and I watch modern-day players who could not lace Chic's boots. I can be sitting there seeing how a game develops and witnessing players making wrong decision after wrong decision. On occasion, I'll nudge Jim and say something like, 'Chic would have hit a reverse pass there' or 'Chic would have switched wings'. Wee points, but ones I believe to be valid. As you will have gathered by now, I always rated Chic as being a special talent. If you asked me to select a particular outstanding individual performance from him I couldn't. Simply put, there were so many. What was the best song ever written by Lennon and McCartney? There are so many to choose from and every individual will have his or her favourite. Chic brought a little sprinkling of gold dust to so many confrontations on a Saturday. He could turn a grey afternoon in Maryhill into an illuminating spectacle. And he did it time and time again. He could do things with a football other players can merely dream about. There are guys out there today earning fortunes and they couldn't trap a bag of cement.

OK, if he was that good, how come he never played at the highest level? Easy answer – he didn't meet the right manager at the important stage of his development right at the start. I am not pointing fingers at anyone here, but how can a youngster such as Chic, after a couple of years on the books of St Mirren and Ayr United, be allowed to drift out football to work on the oil rigs for three years? His ability was there for all to see and he really needed someone to sort him out early on. That was the important part of his career. Aye, I am aware he liked a pint or two with his mates from Possil, but someone should have had the strength of character to deal with such things and emphasise to a teenager what he could achieve in the game with a bit more application and dedication. It's a real pity that didn't happen. Players with only a fraction of his ability went on to have good careers and even won international caps.

It's unbelievable that Chic didn't make a solitary appearance for his country. Totally mystifying. I went along to Scotland games and would see someone playing in Chic's position. Again I would turn to my good friend Jim Oliver and say, 'Chic would have done so much better.' He never got the opportunity and that surely could only be down to SFA bosses being afraid of his reputation. They should have been doing their jobs properly and concentrating completely on the lad's ability. Och, don't get me started on the Largs Mafia. It's not a case of what you know, but who you know. I'm convinced of that. Any other country would have been only too delighted to welcome Chic into their international squad. Aye, even Brazil. Chic could have mixed in any company when he put his mind to it.

As a player, Chic Charnley was special. As a person, Chic Charnley is equally special. As I pointed out right at the start, I'm proud to say he is like a son to me.

INTRODUCTION

Hindsight is a wonderful thing. Unfortunately, it's absolutely bloody useless. If I had the opportunity to travel back in time I would, without hesitation, change about ninety-five per cent of my career. Believe me, it hurts to admit that. Meet the guy who was allergic to making good decisions. I've called it wrong so many times and I blame no-one but myself. If I was dropped in the Sahara Desert and there was one landmine you could put your last five pence on me parachuting right on top of the damn thing. Sometimes I have been in the wrong place at the wrong time, but I'll always hold up my hands when I've made an error. Regrets? I've had a few million.

Please don't get the impression I am looking for anyone's sympathy. Far from it. I accept I should have achieved so much more in my career. That I didn't is purely my fault. No-one else's. I can look back and wonder what might have been, but, as hopefully you will discover in this book, there have been plenty of wonderful moments, treasured memories and madcap happenings. There have been tears, but there have been a few laughs, too. It's taken me a long and winding road to get here and in reaching this part of my life I've learned a lot, that's for sure. They say you should learn from your mistakes. That being the case, I must be the most educated individual on the planet.

As a Glaswegian, born and bred, I've been labelled as a bit of a character. I've even heard I have achieved some sort of cult status. My off-the-field activities seem to be discussed about as much as what I achieved on a football field. All good stories. And some of them are true!

I'm from the Glasgow housing estate of Possil and it's a part of the universe that will never be mistaken for Monte Carlo. By the same token, as far as I am aware, it hasn't been twinned with hell either.

They breed them tough in Possil and you have to learn very quickly to look after yourself. Don't get the impression it is populated mainly by undesirables because there are a lot decent people living there. Simply put, fate has dictated, for whatever reason, this is where they will spend a percentage – or all – of their lives. However, it would also be fair to say I have had – and still have – acquaintances who may not be choirboys, but I don't believe Quentin Tarantino based the film *Reservoir Dogs* on these guys, either. Possil, like other big Glasgow housing schemes such as Castlemilk, Easterhouse, Drumchapel and the like, can be the butt of some cruel humour. Is it true the place is so terrifying that even Rottweilers go around in pairs? What do you call a female in a white shellsuit? The bride. What do you call the guy in the suit, shirt and tie? The accused. The people are so skint that when one of their kids asks for a musical instrument for Christmas they are taught how to whistle. You get the drift.

Glasgow is a wonderful city of rumour and counter-rumour. I've been on the receiving end of some storylines that are more than just a shade fanciful. Some may even be hurtful, but then I console myself with the fact that if there are people out there having a go at me then they will be leaving some others alone. I'm not Peter Perfect and I have never claimed to be – what you see is what you get with me. However, some of the tall tales about yours truly have gained skyscraper status. If even half of them were true I would not be here to write this book in the first place. The authorities would have been opening up Alcatraz just for me! And, no, I have never played in a game where there have been rivers of vodka/whisky/gin/rum/sherry running through me.

Anyway, I don't think anyone out there has to fabricate any stories about me because I'm certain, as I have demonstrated so capably and so consistently over the years, I have provided enough material myself without having to deal in fiction. For a start, I've seen more than a few red cards in my career – seventeen in total – and there have been so many training bust-ups with team-mates that I've lost count. I've gone head-to-head and toe-to-toe with a few bosses, too. I've also had four stints at Partick Thistle and people wonder why I take a pint! Would you believe I was only ever ordered off twice in my days as a Firhill player? One of them, as I will tell you later in the book, was a complete injustice.

On my twenty-year trek through football – I started at nineteen and finished at thirty-nine – I've also played for Ayr United, Clydebank, Hamilton Accies, Dumbarton, Dundee and Hibs. I had a brief loan spell at Bolton Wanderers and a stint in Sweden with Djurgardens. There was a spell with Irish outfit Portadown as well as seasons in the Juniors with Pollok, Tarff Rovers and Kirkintilloch Rob Roy. Oh, and did I mention I also played for a team called Celtic? It was only once, but I can assure you I will never forget that occasion. No way.

I'm also the bloke that the late, great Jim Baxter, of Rangers and Scotland fame, once remarked, 'See that Charnley – he's one of the only players I would bother to turn up to watch play.' There was another occasion when Hibs legend Eddie Turnbull was being interviewed on television and he said, 'Chic Charnley has more ability in his big toe than most players possess in their entire being.'

It's time for the real Chic Charnley to stand up and have his say. Let's find out if I am really the wild man of Scottish foot-ball. Let's discover if people were frightened away from taking a chance on me because of my reputation. Am I as bad as I've been painted? Could I really have done all those things, on and off the field, and still be alive to tell the tale? Talking earlier about film director Tarantino, I had to laugh when John Colquhoun, the former Celtic and Hearts winger, once said to me, 'Do you know, Chic, watching you is like watching a Tarantino movie – you just know at some point something is going to happen.' Whatever does he mean?

I read a piece by a journalist that stated I had 'a voracious appetite for trouble'. What a thing to say. Now if I meet that guy he might just get a slap! Only joking. Anyway, fasten your safety belts, please, we're in for a bumpy ride . . .

1

HERE WE GO!

James Callaghan Charnley made his debut on Earth at Glasgow's Oakbank Hospital on 11 June 1963, the second son to Isa and John and named after my uncle. Edward arrived a year before me and Angela twelve months afterwards. Anne, John, Margaret and Frank completed the family as the Charnley clan grew as the years rolled by. Home was Killearn Street, Possil in the north of Glasgow, a place where you had to have an honours degree in the University of Life to survive and succeed.

I spent many happy years with my granny Agnes, who stayed in the same street. I loved that lady and, in typical Glaswegian fashion, she would give you her last. I saw her do it time and time again. A neighbour would come to the door asking if we had any milk to spare. 'Aye, we've got lots,' she would say and hand out a half-full bottle. There would be no milk left in the house. She had done it again. Her acts of kindness became legendary where she lived and I'm sure everyone thought the world of her. I know I did. I never needed any persuading to nip round to see her. There was method in my madness, of course. For a start, there were plenty of other Charnleys at home for Ma – I could never call her mum or mother – and Da – I could never call him dad or father – to take care of. I had my granny all to myself and vice versa. I was well looked after by this lovely woman. She was a charming lady I will remember for the rest of my life. My Ma used to have to drag me screaming and bawling when it was time to go home. I was physically dragged along the road on some occasions.

My granny was also a genuine character. Would you believe she went to her first Old Firm game when she was over sixty years old? Remarkable! A friend, Phillip Dougan, ran the Round Toll supporters' bus and he persuaded my dear old gran to go to Ibrox one day to support Celtic against Rangers. She didn't even hesitate as she agreed to go into 'enemy territory' for the first time. Sadly, this wonderful lady passed away in 1988 at the age of sixty-nine. I still miss her and I always will. She brought so many good things to my life and I will be forever grateful.

My granda Bill was a real card. He once came to watch me play for Hamilton and disappeared after twenty minutes when he discovered the bar at the social club was open! An uncle gave him a bottle of whisky to share with another uncle. Needless to say my granda tanned the lot. He was asked for an explanation: 'I had to drink his half to get to my half,' he responded. Argue with that!

Undoubtedly, Possil was a tough area to live and grow up in, but I met so many good families in that environment. I'm talking about the Cadberrys, Redmonds, Olivers, Gaughans and many more. People who could look after themselves, but good people to have around you. When you made a friend in that part of the world you had a genuine friend for life. There was no place for phonies in that environment.

OK, you might be wondering why someone nicknamed Chic was christened James. People have often referred to me as Charles, but I always assume they're talking about someone else. I don't see myself as a Charles, do you? So, let's enlighten everyone at long last. I had a relative who worked in a place where he could, ahem, 'acquire' frozen chickens. He would bring them home with him and give them to me to sell round the doors of the estate. I would knock on the doors of the neighbours and enquire, 'Chicken?' If they were flush, they might even buy a couple. If they were skint, it would be, 'Maybe tomorrow.' I was just a kid, about nine years old, when I traipsed around the tenements of Possil with just poultry for company. You soon got to know who had cash on such-and-such a day. A lot of people were paid in readies on a weekly basis back then. Some would get their wages on a Monday or a Tuesday or whatever. These were the houses first on the radar when I had my wares to sell. The quicker I sold them, the quicker I could join my mates for a kickabout.

In time, I became known as Little Chicken, the wee boy who sells chickens at your door. My Ma did not care for that particular monniker. 'If you're going to call him anything, then call him Chic,' she told the neighbours. In time, that's what they did and I am delighted for my Ma's intervention. Otherwise you'd be reading a book by Little Chicken Charnley! Sounds as though I should be the frontman for a Mississippi Delta Blues Band. Actually, there was a bloke in the neighbourhood called John Gaughan who obviously saw himself as a bit of an artist. He took out a brush and paint one day and scrawled an enormous message on a wall that said simply, 'Wee Chicken Charnley.' He then painted what he thought looked like a chicken. I suppose it was some sort of advertising although I'm pretty sure the local council authorities weren't too pleased.

I did all sorts of odd jobs as I was growing up. My Da appeared to be a bit of a Jack-of-all-trades and bounced from one job to another. My Ma, as I recall, worked every day in jobs all over the place. I'm sure she held down three jobs at one stage. I recall she once worked in a chemist's shop in Saracen Street in Glasgow. She also had a post in Ruchill Hospital. What a woman. She is still extremely active and I popped in one morning to see her on one of those rarest of days – a hot summer's day in 2009. She

3

was trying to shift one of these huge mahogany wardrobes on her own. She was puffing and panting as she came to the door. 'Son, I'm roasting,' she said. I replied, 'Well, Ma, you could take off one of those cardigans!'

Like a lot of the people my Da worked with and grew up alongside, he was partial to a wee bevvy every now and again. Well, mainly when there was a 'y' in the day. At one point he sold the Glasgow evening newspapers, the *Evening Times* and the now-defunct *Citizen*, at the corner of West Nile Street and Bath Street. It was a busy junction, as I recall, and he took me along once to show me the ropes. I wondered if one day it would be my pitch.

He taught me how to fold the newspaper expertly and fire it under the buyer's armpit as the money was handed over. Every now and again a generous commuter would say, 'Keep the change.' My Da's 'workplace' just happened to be beside a pub called the Bay Horse, no longer there, alas. The location could have been a complete coincidence, of course. On that particular day, my Da would say, 'Right, James, you take over, I'm just going in to use the toilet. I'll be back in a minute.' I didn't own a wristwatch back then, but I'm fairly certain my dad was missing longer than sixty seconds when he popped into the bar. Then we went home and my Da said, 'Isa, what a day I've had!' Unfortunately, my Da passed away in his early fifties. He didn't get a fair kick of the ball.

I escaped from school at sixteen years old. I couldn't stand the place and was desperate to get out into the big wide world. I met some good friends at my primary and secondary schools. Joe Sutherland, nicknamed Stud for some reason, was a pal and he was absolutely crazy. Honestly, this bloke made me look sane and that is no easy task. I remember a day when we were sitting in class and the teacher had her back to us as she chalked something on the blackboard. Stud produced this light bulb from

4

somewhere and, without warning, fired it at the blackboard. It smashed just above the teacher's head and she almost passed out. God, it gave me a fright and I was sitting beside him! Such an action wasn't out of the ordinary for Stud. In fact, in time you started to expect the unexpected from him. His mum was called Mary and she worked in the local chippy, or fish and chip shop, if you want to be posh. What a bonus that was. Stud and I made regular visits to her place of work, as you might imagine, and we gorged ourselves with everything we could get our hands on. I wonder if that chippy ever made a profit!

Frank Redmond, known as Bogy, was my best mate. He was a fantastic footballer, a lot better than me, but he didn't attempt to pursue it has a career when he left school. My Uncle William married Bogy's sister and I found it strange calling her Auntie!

Another good chum was John Hynd. I'll tell you a story about him in another chapter. He was known as Hyndo to everyone – were we an imaginative lot in Possil or what? – but he also had a nickname, Nae Cash. I remember meeting up with him in a pub one night. I had just come back from a holiday in Florida and had picked up a bit of a suntan. I wore all white that night to emphasise my new look. Hyndo was at the bar and he was dressed all in black. I looked at him and said, 'Hyndo, you look just like Johnny Cash.' He pulled out both his pockets and they were empty. 'You mean Johnny Nae Cash, don't you?' The nickname stuck.

I recall two teachers, Mr McKee and Mr McRae – I never did know their first names – who took charge of the St Theresa's football team. I still see Mr McKee when I'm out jogging these days and I spot him regularly at Celtic Park on matchdays, too. Mr McRae was probably the first bloke to ever send me off. He was really strict about never belittling your opponents, but, as kids, we couldn't stop ourselves from showing off a bit, especially after scoring a goal. You would whack one past the rival keeper and run away shouting 'Easy!' Mr McRae was not amused. I was hauled off on more than one occasion and replaced by a team-mate. Och, I was only having some harmless fun.

That's more than can be said for the older lads at St Augustine's school, the one I would join later on. You had to tread carefully around the Milton those days. You also had to be a very good runner around that time because, just to pass the time, these guys liked nothing better than to chase you down the road after a game. I always got the impression it was not to congratulate us on our performance that day. It didn't matter if you had won, drawn or lost – you knew these blokes would be waiting for you. So, it was a case of getting ready as quickly as possible and making sure you had your best trainers on your feet. The St Augustine's mob would assemble outside and then, with a swift opening of the door, we all fled in the general direction of home. If you were lucky, you might even catch a bus while the baying horde behind you screamed all sorts of threats. Then, when I went to St Augustine's, it was my turn to run with the rabble and chase opposing players all over the place. I got caught by a teacher once after we had played a team called St Cuthberts. A lot of us were caught, in fact, and I served my first-ever football suspension. I was banned for a week!

I also played for St Theresa's Boys' Guild. The team was run by two blokes, Eddie Brady and Charlie McKenna. Like a lot of people, they put in their time and effort for nothing. They were simply football fans and were doing their best for the local community. Guys like that are gold dust. I remember Willie Carr played for the side and he went onto have a great career in the seniors. He played for years with Coventry City and was capped six times for the Scotland international side. As usual, there was a bit of good-natured rivalry at the Boys' Guild and two brothers, Willie and Peter Kerr, and Con Dillon, who were about ten years older than us, used to keep our feet on the ground by continually reminding us that they had played in the side that had won the John Thomson Trophy, a much sought-after trophy at that level. 'Come back and talk to us about football when you've got some medals to show us, lads.'

After leaving school, I was given a job at Littlewoods Warehouse where I met a lovely girl called Margaret. It was her first job, too, and eventually we stuck up a rapport. We married and she gave me two wonderful children in Gary and Danielle.

While I was still at Littlewoods I went part-time with St Mirren and, thankfully, had a very kind relation in Uncle William who would pick me up after my day's work and drive me through to Love Street for training. This went on for about four or five months and, once again, I knew I was fortunate to have such a great family around me. I also had an Uncle James who was another character. He actually boxed and skied for the army and was berthed in Germany. However, he was Celtic daft and tried to get to Parkhead as often as possible. He recalled watching Celtic play Yugoslav outfit Vojvodina Novi Sad in the European Cup quarter-final in 1967. Celtic had lost the first leg 1-0 and there was no way my uncle was going to miss the return. The Hoops duly won 2-0 to go through and, of course, they eventually conquered Europe in May of that year. He recalled going back to Germany and all he could still hear ringing in his ears was, 'Celtic . . . Celtic.'

Uncle John was a remarkable individual. Honestly, he did the daftest things. My granny stayed in the top floor flat in a tenement in Killearn Street. It was three storeys high, but Uncle John had a strange way of entering the front room – via the window. When he was drunk he must have thought he was a mountaineer and would climb up the drainpipe. Obviously, it would have been too easy for him to use the stairs. You could be sitting watching the television when suddenly this head would emerge at the window. Uncle John had arrived. We were all terrified that he would do himself a mischief some day, especially as he was half-pissed most of the time, but, amazingly, he was never hurt. He made it every time. It must have been an interesting sight for the neighbours across the road to see my Uncle John doing his impression of Spiderman after sinking a few in the local boozer. Interesting man, my Uncle John!

2

IN THE BEGINNING

You may be surprised to discover that I didn't play football for my secondary school team St Augustine's in Milton. Then again, my detractors may not! I think I turned out for the school twice in three years and there was a very good reason for that – I was too busy following Celtic. Obviously, I loved kicking the ball about and could be found out on the streets most nights with my mates annoying the neighbours. If the school team had played on any other day other than a Saturday I would have been delighted to represent St Augustine's. But that particular day was saved for supporting the Bhoys.

I had played for my primary school, St Theresa's in Possil, but I hung up my boots at a very early age to get behind Celtic. Nothing else seemed to matter. A chap called Peter Quinn ran a fifty-seater coach and he used to take the supporters to games in exotic places such as Dundee, Fife and Edinburgh. I really liked him and he would always give me two bob – ten pence these days – when he dropped me off at home. I recall going with the rest of the fans to watch Celtic against Dunfermline at East End Park one Saturday. I was about six or seven years old at the time and, as I recall, Celtic won and scored three goals. However, I was mystified during the match. My heroes were playing in an all-green strip. I had never seen them wear that outfit before. What had happened to those wonderful green and white hoops? Someone had to explain the colour clash with Dunfermline, but I have to say I still prefer to see Celtic in the hoops.

There were was one absolutely unforgettable incident when I went with the bus to see Celtic play Ayr United at Somerset Park. I was just a kid and my pals raced onto the pitch to celebrate after Celtic had scored a goal. There I was, cavorting around the playing surface, when I felt this huge hand on my shoulder. I thought it was a cop and I had been nicked. Could you imagine my surprise when I looked round and there was none other than Jock Stein himself telling me, 'Come on, son, that's enough of that. Off you go.' I almost fainted. Big Jock had touched me. He had even spoken to me. I was in heaven.

Talking of fainting, I did feign the dying swan act every now and again at Celtic Park. Those were the days the St John's ambulancemen would take you out of the crowd and walk you round the trackside and past the dug-outs. I would sneak a look at Big Jock and the substitutes. I would do anything just to get close to those guys. Mind you, the ambulancemen must have thought I was a fragile wee soul as I appeared to pass out every matchday at Parkhead. Wee Jimmy Johnstone was my hero. Everyone loved him and I would travel everywhere to witness those fascinating skills. Jinky was simply sublime and was everything I loved in a footballer. His touch was wonderful, his vision was something else altogether and, of course, he could launch those mesmerising runs at terrified defenders. He was afraid of no-one or anything. He might have been five feet nothing, but, put that ball at his feet, and he was a giant among men.

I can always recall a deadly hush sweeping around the Rangers end in Old Firm games when the ball went to Jinky. They were petrified at what our wee genius might conjure up. He had a bit of a temper, too, I seem to recall. I think we had quite a bit in common! Actually, what I loved most about Jinky was his enter-

10

tainment value. I know football is big business and corporate giants have massive financial stakes in clubs, but I still believe you should entertain the fans. That seems to be largely forgotten these days and that's a shame. I've got a lot of pals who aren't exactly rolling in cash, but they will always get their hands on enough to take them to see their team in action on matchday. It's their special day and as soon as the final whistle has gone they are looking forward to next week's game. It's so important to them and their loyalty is quite incredible. They deserve to see something special and they are due a wee bit of magic from some individuals. Jinky provided that. Always. I loved watching him at work and he always seemed to play football the way it was intended to be played.

I recall an amazing night with Jinky when we teamed up on stage at The Mayfair Club in Glasgow. The main act was an Irish band called The Peatdiggers. The compere took the microphone at one point and announced to the audience that a certain Jimmy Johnstone was in attendance. The Wee Man, as you might expect, got a rapturous welcome. Then, to my astonishment, the compere told the punters that Chic Charnley was also at the gig. I got a great reception, too, and before I knew it I was up on stage with my all-time sporting hero. They made the mistake of asking Jinky and I to belt out some songs. We were giving some Celtic and Irish songs laldy. We were having so much fun that they had to eventually throw us off the stage!

When I started turning out for Possil Villa, an amateur team who played in the Glasgow Suburban League, I used to have my socks around my ankles. People often asked me why I adopted this style and the answer was easy – that's the way Jinky used to have his socks. I was copying him. Later the fuddy-duddies who rule football passed a regulation that players must have their socks pulled up to their knees and shinguards were compulsory, too, whether you wanted them or not. I had to comply with

11

the rules as I didn't want to get into trouble with the referees! A bloke called John Bell ran Possil and he made sure we had the best of strips, boots and all the gear. It made you feel as though you were already in the big-time.

My eyes were opened playing at this level. I recall an incident in a pub the night before a game on the Saturday. There was a wee fall-out between a guy called Alex Forbes and my mate Podgy, real name George Lyttle. It was nothing serious, but I soon discovered that my pal had the ability to bear a grudge. During the game he went to take a shy and motioned for Alex to come over to head the throw-in back to him. Alex must have thought they had become instant friends again. He was to find out differently seconds later. He didn't see Podgy rubbing the ball on some dog dirt that was on the touchline. He covered the ball in shit and then tossed it for Alex. Splat! Alex's head made contact with the offending article. Poo was running down his face and he must have thought it was water. He wiped some of it away with his hand when the full horror struck him. He saw the shit and simply walked off the pitch and went home. I don't suppose he saw the funny side. I'm not sure I would have, either, come to think about it.

There was the little matter of taking care of scholastic duties, of course, before I could escape into the real world to pursue my love of football. During my time at school my so-called chums told me I had a large head and called me 'Heid'. Very original! I think the guy sitting directly behind me was marked absent for the first three years of his schooldays! But I'm glad it didn't stick.

It would be fair to say I didn't enjoy schooldays. Whoever said they were the best days of your life got that a hundred per cent wrong, as far as I am concerned. I wasn't the school dunce or anything like that, but my attention span wasn't great and I couldn't hold facts that I didn't believe would help me when I left school. OK, that's not what I have preached to my daughter Danielle or my son Gary, but, back then, the only thing I wanted to do was play football. Who cared how many sides there were on an opaque? So what if X over Y equalled Z in algebra? I can't count the amount of times I failed my maths test. It just didn't seem to be important.

I can remember being totally embarrassed one day when I was in art class. I couldn't draw a circle even if you put a gun to my head. Anyway, we were given this test and, as you might expect, my attempt at painting flowers in a vase looked a bit more like an explosion in a dye works. The art teacher wasn't impressed. He marched me out in front of the class and, basically, made a fool of me. I felt my face go crimson as he showed off my work to the rest of the class. The more they laughed, the more I felt like finding a hole and crawling into it. Why on earth would an adult belittle someone in such a horrible way? I couldn't draw to save myself, but that was the best I could do. Yes, it was rubbish, but that was simply because I did not have an artistic touch. Maybe I should have used my left foot – I might have had more success. But I'll always remember that day. According to that particular teacher the only thing that should be hanging in the Art Gallery should be James Charnley. By the neck. I hated him for that and if I could duck out of art classes for any reason then I did.

Football, though, did hold my concentration. My mates and I used to play a game called 'heady-footy' where you could head the ball and then volley it before it hit the ground. It was one against one and whoever scored the first goal stayed in the game and another opponent came in to play you. I made sure I played as long as possible because if I was knocked out I had to join a queue of other kids waiting their turn to get back in again. We only ever had one ball, so there was only one game. And if you were out you could be on the sidelines for about half an hour.

I never fancied that. I practised my skills night and day and it's because of this backyard game that I honed my skills. It also helped you to become a winner.

So, my first move was to Possil Villa and then I stepped up into the Juniors and quickly discovered you had to look after yourself in this arena. Luckily enough, I had been able to do so from a very early age. I remember playing for our street team when I was about eight or nine years old and I would be up against adults, some of them were even married men. I was by far the youngest on the pitch and the opposition didn't observe the niceties of the game. I would hear cries from their players along the lines of, 'Kick that little bastard.' It didn't matter you were just a kid. They would try to boot you all over the place. So, moving into the world of Juniors was an interesting one for me but not too terrifying.

Ironically, it was a guy I used to cheer on from the Parkhead terracings who spotted me and insisted Rutherglen Glencairn sign me. It was Willie O'Neill, who was the Celtic left-back in the first four games of their glorious European Cup run in 1967. He played in the ties against Swiss club Zurich and French outfit Nantes and Celtic won them all. However, Big Jock changed things around by the time the quarter-final against Yugoslav team Vojvodina Novi Sad came round and switched Tommy Gemmell to left-back and brought in Jim Craig on the right. The rest, as they say, is history.

But Willie O'Neill certainly knew how to spot a player! Glencairn was a breeding ground for young talent and there was always a posse of scouts at our games. It was the ideal launching pad to the seniors. We had a guy up front who was making a bit of a name for himself called Jas Carbin who had scored four goals against former Celtic goalkeeper Denis Connaghan in one game. I accept Denis was at the veteran stage of his career, but he was still a top-class shotstopper in the Juniors back in 1981.

In fact, he had played for Celtic in the European Cup seven years beforehand against Greek side Olympiakos, so that will tell you something about his pedigree. Hammering four behind him was a marvellous feat by Jas and, as you might expect, some senior clubs sent scouts to a few of our games afterwards to check his progress.

Someone at Hamilton must have been impressed by yours truly because I was invited along to their old Douglas Park ground and boss Davie McParland gave me a trial in a game against St Mirren. I must have done well enough because Accies asked me to sign for them. But the next thing I heard was that Hearts wanted to have me over at Tynecastle for a week as they were eager to have a look.

Manager Alex MacDonald must have been keen because he travelled through to Possil to meet me. My Ma wanted to take MacDonald into the front room, but I insisted we conducted business in my bedroom. As we all know, Alex was a former Rangers player and, like me, never tried to disguise his allegiance to his particular half of the Old Firm divide. That was fine by me, but Alex came close to going weak at the knees when he saw my bedroom. Actually, it was more of a shrine to all things Celtic. There were my heroes' photographs and all sorts of memorabilia plastered all over the walls. There was no escape because the Hearts boss was also standing on a Celtic carpet!

To be fair to Alex, it didn't faze him too much and he made me the offer to go through to Tynecastle for seven days. When I got there, he introduced me to his co-manager Sandy Jardine, another ex-Rangers player, and he said, 'You should see this guy's bedroom. He's got more Celtic things in there than there are at Celtic Park!' I was working in a Littlewoods warehouse in Glasgow at the time and I was desperate to break into the seniors. I worked hard at Hearts for a week and thought I had done reasonably well. I played in one reserve game where John

Robertson scored an excellent hat-trick. Anyway, Sandy Jardine gave me a lift back in his car from training one night. I thought it was a nice gesture and his stock rose very swiftly in my eyes when he asked if I wanted to go for a pint. I was nineteen years old and, after a fairly gruelling training session, was right in the mood for a beer or two.

A beer or two became five or six and Sandy realised the club's teenage trainee had a thirst for even more. I don't think the Tynecastle co-gaffer was greatly impressed. If it was meant to be a test, then I had failed. I wasn't going to kid the guy and have a Babycham, was I? I enjoyed a beer and I wasn't going to disguise it. Anyway, I always felt fit and worked hard in training, so any excesses from the previous evening would be taken care of the following morning. OK, I realise this did not make me an ideal role model for any youngster wishing to become a professional footballer, but it was the way I was and it was a case of like it or lump it. I stayed with an aunt in Dalkeith during the week I was on trial with Hearts, but I was told they would not be following up on their initial interest. Apparently, they were 'looking for someone more experienced'. Perhaps they believed I would age about three years during my seven-day spell with them.

However, it wasn't long before I did move into the seniors. St Mirren had noticed something in me during my trial for Hamilton and it was off to Love Street for the first of my two stints at the Paisley outfit. I was signed by Ricky McFarlane, but when he left during the season it didn't take long for Alex Miller to take a dislike to me. The feeling was mutual.

3

NO LOVE AT LOVE STREET

I have never received a Christmas card from Alex Miller, my old manager at St Mirren. I've got a pretty good idea why – I don't suppose you should go around throwing boots at your gaffer!

It was nearing the end of my first season as a senior footballer and, although I wasn't aware of it at the time, I was also edging closer to the exit door at Love Street. I had got on really well with Miller's predecessor Ricky McFarlane while a bloke called Eddie McDonald used to take the reserves. It was a joy to play for these two guys. Obviously, I can't say the same for Miller. It's not just that we weren't on the same wavelength, we weren't on the same planet. He just didn't take to me and he didn't seem to like the company I kept – Frank McAvennie and Frank McDougall!

The three of us used to travel through to Paisley in the same car and we had a reputation for fooling around. The two Franks were a few years older than me and were already in the first team. I was still awaiting my opportunity and I admit I had an awful lot to learn about being a professional footballer. Before Miller arrived, we played for the reserve team and Eddie McDonald once told me he would pay me £5 if I could score direct from a corner-kick. 'What if I can score two?' I enquired rather cockily. 'I'll make it £10,' he said. I'll bet he wished he'd kept his mouth shut. I duly stepped up to take the first corner, bent it beautifully with my left foot and the ball flew past a bemused goalkeeper. 'That's a fiver you owe me, Eddie,' I shouted over to the bench. He nodded his head. We got another corner later in the game and, yes, lightning can strike twice in the same place. I glanced at the bench and shouted over, 'Have that tenner ready by the end of the game.' This time he grimaced. I placed the ball in the arc, surveyed the situation, curled it again with my left peg and, lo and behold, the frantic keeper was left clutching at thin air as my effort sailed into the net once again. Good old Eddie. He paid up.

Alex Miller was a different sort of guy altogether. He always looked glum, with hunched shoulders. He would have made a great Rigsby in the TV comedy *Rising Damp*. He had the haunted look of a guy heading for the gallows. Someone must have told him they had slapped a tax on smiling. I remembered him as a player with Rangers and I didn't rate him at all. I didn't think he could pass the ball, for a start, and that's a bit of a drawback for any footballer. He was now making his way in the game as a manager and he was deadly serious about going all the way to the top. St Mirren were obviously a stepping stone to bigger and better things.

He and his assistant Drew Jarvie spent most of their time frowning about this, that and the next thing. There was an evening when Macca, Frank and I went out to a bar in Paisley and were having a couple of drinks and a natter. Suddenly McAvennie and McDougall straightened up and, when it was my turn to get them in, they both asked for orange juices. I said, 'You're joking. Orange juices? Are you both ill?' They assured me that's what they fancied and I went to the bar, more than just a little bit puzzled by the sudden attack of alcohol abstinence by my colleagues.

I duly ordered up their orange juices and got myself my tipple at the time, a vodka and coke. As I carried the drinks back to our table I glanced up and sitting immediately behind us were Miller and Jarvie. My two mates, the rotten swines, hadn't even tipped me off. Our managerial double act didn't look too impressed with me and no doubt Macca and McDougall, making sure our bosses spotted their fruit juices, got gold stars in their jotters. I made my debut for the club four months after signing for them. It was against Hibs at Easter Road on New Year's Day 1983. My first touch was to push the ball through the legs of their defender Mike Conroy. He wasn't impressed and clattered me. Welcome to senior football, Chic! It ended goalless and, to be honest, wasn't much of a spectacle, but it was great to be involved. Ricky McFarlane showed great faith in me and I'll never forget that.

The end was nigh, though, on the day when I came in from training and Miller ordered me to clean the boots. I thought I had misheard him. I queried, 'Sorry? You want me to do what?' He ordered, 'Clean everyone's boots. Get on with it.' Now I saw myself as a professional footballer at the time, trying to make a name for myself. But here I was being told I was to become a boot-boy. Frankly, I would have eaten broken glass before I took on that task. The trigger went off in my head. I picked up a couple of particularly muddy boots and fired them at a startled Miller. 'Clean them your fuckin' self,' I barked. I wasn't offered a new contract at the end of the season. That came as a surprise!

Then it was off to Ayr United where George Caldwell was the manager. I enjoyed myself at Somerset Park although, of course, I missed the day-to-day company of my two amigos, McAvennie and McDougall. However, I still found time to socialise away from Paisley. There was one Sunday afternoon when myself and a pal decided to go on a bender. I must have been celebrating a good result the previous day because I really went at it with a fair degree of verve and gusto. We weren't annoying anyone and there was no trouble, but we were very quickly getting legless.

We were just two young guys having a good time in Possil. We just kept sticking them away and, as the hours ticked by, we might have realised we needed more bevvy like a drowning man needed a glass of water.

After a few visits to some of the local pubs we stumbled out into the street. I stress there was no bother, but two passing policemen weren't too impressed by our condition. They stopped us in our tracks. One took me by the arm and said, 'Right, you, let's take you down to the cells. You can sleep it off.' Bleary-eyed, I squinted at him and said, 'You can't do that. I'm Chic Charnley and I play for Ayr United.' He didn't even crack a smile as he replied, 'Look, son, George Best has just done three months and he plays for Manchester United!' How can you argue with that? They took us down the nick and let us go without charge when we sobered up. If memory serves correctly that was sometime late the following day.

I played seventeen games for Ayr and scored three goals, but by the end of that first season at the club I came to a momentous decision. I was going to quit football.

4

LIFE ON THE RIGS

When I decided to leave Ayr United in 1984 I thought my career in senior football was over, at the age of twenty-one. I couldn't have guessed that I would make another twelve moves to senior clubs – four to Partick Thistle – enjoy spells in Sweden and Ireland, have a loan stint at Bolton Wanderers and spend four years in the Juniors with three different teams.

A pal called Jim Carruthers, who used to work on the oil rigs in Nairn, ran a football team and got in touch to see if I would be interested in coming up to work with him. Actually, I have to admit that I didn't do a day's turn for him. He just wanted me to play in his weekend league side. If I remember correctly, I agreed to £400-per-week in wages. 'I'm desperate to win the league up here, Chic,' he told me. 'With you in the team we might just have a chance.'

Johnny Hamilton, who played for Rangers and Hibs, was also in the line-up and I decided to take a chance. I had nothing to lose because very little was opening up for me in Glasgow. It looked as though my fledgling football career was over before it had begun. I was still young, of course, and packed my bags to go up north to see if I could help my mate win the local title. I have to say Jim should be applauded for taking about twenty other guys from Possil off the dole. He gave them all a variety of jobs up on the rigs. I was out of the senior game for three years, but enjoyed myself in Nairn with a good bunch of lads. It was an interesting time. We used to travel up on a Sunday morning usually around 3am and our shift started at 10am. Johnny Hamilton was the ganger and in charge of the workers.

I clocked in, but didn't do anything other than play for the team on a Sunday afternoon. We were onshore and I remember we had to put on these overalls to look the part just in case a boss turned up. I used to enjoy a wee nap in the toilets. There were about thirty cubicles on the site and the snoring from the rest of the lads must have sounded like buzz saws to anyone walking past. I remember one day when Johnny was doing his rounds and he decided to pop into the loo to flush out – no pun intended – some of the shirkers. He knocked on my door and awakened me from my slumber. Still half asleep, I got to my feet and Johnny asked, 'What are you doing in there?' I put on my best innocent look and replied, 'I'm having a leak.' Johnny looked at me and laughed, 'Well, try to undo your overalls when you're doing the toilet or you will make a right fuckin' mess.' On another occasion Johnny asked one of my pals, 'And what have you done today?' Quick as a flash came the reply, 'Oh, about four cans and a half-bottle!'

Jim Carruthers, who has remained a good friend to this day, struck a deal with me. 'Chic,' he said, 'you score a hat-trick in a game and I promise to drive you back to Glasgow right after the match. OK?' He probably thought he would be safe because I wasn't a noted goalscorer, but in that league I knew I could do the business. 'You've got a deal,' I answered. As I recall, I rattled in about four or five hat-tricks, but Jim, always desperate to get one over the local teams, never grumbled once as we headed back to Glasgow. And we won the league, too.

I used to play for a pub team, as well, called Rockerfellers, which was owned by another pal. A former Kilmarnock player called Jimmy Hughes took me aside one day and said, 'What are you doing? You're too good for this league. You should still be playing at senior level.' As luck would have it, the contract at the oil rigs was coming to an end so I would have been looking for new employment anyway. Jimmy put a call in to a guy called Dickie Brock, who was manager of Pollok Juniors. We got together, Dickie gave me £4,000 for signing for his club and I was up and running once more. Dickie was brilliant to me and gave me a lot of assistance and guidance. Jimmy Hughes, too, deserves massive credit for offering me help when I most needed it.

I still laugh at the memory of Jimmy in the dressing room one day after he had a night out on the bevvy the previous evening. He was holding court telling all the players how much alcohol he had demolished the night before. 'I was so drunk I even drove my car,' said Jimmy. 'I remember taking the wing mirror off this big black car when I crashed into it.' He described in fair detail where and when the accident had taken place. We were all having a laugh with one exception, a guy called Jim Gillespie. 'That was my fuckin' car,' he exclaimed as Jimmy ran for cover.

There was a lot of fun, too, at Rutherglen Glencairn. Well, there would be with a bloke like Willie O'Neill around. He knew I was Celtic daft and I would annoy the life out of him asking about what it was like to play for Jock Stein. What was it like to line up with a genius like Jimmy Johnstone? What was it like playing against Rangers in an Old Firm Cup Final? This would go on endlessly and Willie would start to tell me a story and, before reaching the conclusion, he would make up some excuse to go elsewhere and leave you hanging. He would reel me in every time. Then, he told me he had received a European Cup winners' medal although, of course, he didn't play in the 1967 final against Inter Milan in Lisbon. However, as I have said in another chapter, he had performed at left-back in the first four ties against Zurich and Nantes. So, a medal was struck for him.

One day he called me over and said, 'Chic, I'm thinking of

23

giving you my European Cup medal. What do you say to that?' There would have been no contest whatsoever if I had the opportunity of choosing between a Lottery win and Willie O'Neill's medal. Willie's prized possession would have won out of the park. 'What would I say, Willie?' I spluttered. 'Thanks very much, for a start!' Willie smiled. 'I'll bring it in for you.' I didn't sleep for about a week and was beside myself in anticipation. I'm still waiting to even see the bloody thing. Willie, as I swiftly found out, had a wicked sense of humour.

Willie had the sort of bandy legs you could fly a Jumbo Jet through. I know there used to be competitions between the Celtic players during training about how many times they could nutmeg their team-mate. I am reliably informed by Bertie Auld that, despite the acres of space between Willie's legs, no-one actually managed it. A few days after the European Cup win in Portugal, Celtic lined up against Real Madrid in the Bernabeu Stadium in the Testimonial Match for the legendary Alfredo di Stefano. Jock Stein made a couple of changes to the side and brought in goalkeeper John Fallon for Ronnie Simpson and Willie for John Clark. Jock once said that his Lisbon team would never be beaten and that's why he selected John and Willie. Alfredo, approaching forty, kicked off and played for about fifteen minutes before being withdrawn. However, in that short spell he managed to do something no Celtic player had achieved in training – he stuck the ball through Willie's legs.

Asked afterwards by his mates about the incident, Willie, stone-faced as usual, replied, 'Ach, 120,000 fans turned out and I wanted to make it a memorable night for Alfredo!'

5

TARFF LUCK

Partick Thistle, Hibs, Dundee, St Mirren, Djurgardens . . . and Tarff Rovers. How on earth did they get onto my CV? Simple answer – cash.

I left Firhill for the third time in 1998, freed after only a handful of games. I was signed by John McVeigh, but, unfortunately, he was sacked near the end of the season. I didn't do myself justice in those rare outings and I certainly didn't do anything like enough to merit a long-term contract. I wondered about my next move when, completely out of the blue, I got a call to go down to the Borders and meet this bloke called Robert Burns, chairman of Tarff Rovers.

He was an exceptionally wealthy young man – I think he was still in his thirties – and I thought it would be only polite to meet him, but I can tell you I had absolutely no intention of signing for his club. I still thought I had a future in the senior game, but my telephone wasn't exactly melting with offers coming in. Anyway, I met with Robert and I was hugely impressed by him. His main ambition, it turned out, was to get Tarff Rovers into the first round proper of the Scottish Cup, something they had never achieved in their history.

Robert outlined his plans for the club and the part he wanted me to play. I was interested when he started talking money. He was willing to give me a £10,000 signing-on fee there and then plus a £400-per-week basic wage. It was a fabulous contract and one that top clubs in the senior divisions would have been hard pushed to match. I didn't hesitate in putting pen to paper.

Back then, Tarff had to play four games before they got into business end of the Scottish Cup. Sure enough, we won the first three matches and then we came up against Dalbeattie Star, I believe. We had beaten them 7-0 in a previous league game and were fairly confident of giving our millionaire chairman his historic breakthrough. Before that I had taken my old Thistle pal Alan Dinnie down to the club and I think there was an offer of something like £300-per-week on the table for my mate. However, it was thought to be unfair on the other players who had got the club to this stage for one of them to step down and let Alan play. Fair enough. However, we were driving home one day when my pal exclaimed, 'If you ever tell anyone I couldn't get a game for Tarff Rovers I'll boot you where it hurts the most!'

We duly turned up for our meeting with Dalbeattie Star and we were odds-on to get through. As I recall, maybe we were a bit too confident, too complacent. Our opponents seized the moment and beat us 1-0. That was the end of my career in the Borders. Robert Burns, as we had agreed, allowed me to move on and my next stop was Ireland with Portadown.

They are seen as a Protestant club in Northern Ireland, but that didn't bother me. I was still earning and I didn't have to spend time at the club. I flew in on a Friday and returned to Scotland immediately after the Saturday game. It was a situation that suited the club and myself. I recall we were warming up before a match against the predominantly Roman Catholic team Cliftonville. I heard this shout from the crowd, 'Hey, Charnley, you're worse than that wee bastard Mo Johnston!'

The inevitable happened in one of my first games for Portadown – yes, I was ordered off. I had persuaded the club's owners to have a look at my old Thistle mate Steve Pittman and he played in that game, too. Anyway, once again, I got involved with an opponent and the ref couldn't flash his red card quickly enough. I trudged off and headed for another early bath. I had no sooner planked my backside in the pool when the dressing room door banged open, almost coming off its hinges. It was Steve – he had just been sent off, too. I don't think the Irish bosses were too enamoured by their Partick Thistle double-act. I was back in Scotland within a year and, at the age of thirty-six, had joined another Junior side, Kirkintilloch Rob Roy. I was there for three seasons and was quite happy with my lot. I can't remember the actual signing-on fee at the time, but it was quite a bit of money. I also agreed a £200-per-week deal. The manager was a bloke called Gordon Wilson, my former captain at Pollok, and he paid half of that amount out of his own pocket.

I recall playing in a particularly rough and tumble encounter for Rob Roy and there was a bloke in the opposition camp who was kicking me all over the place. It was as though he had a point to prove. Anyway, I tolerated this for about an hour and then he booted me again. Enough was enough. I picked up the ball and was about to fire it into his face when I took a sudden attack of brains. I stopped myself just in time. The referee was mightily impressed. He sidled up to me and said, 'Chic, if you had done that twenty years ago you wouldn't have a sending-off record the length of yourself.' I was learning all the time.

I thought that was the end of the seniors for me until, remarkably, I received a call from John Lambie one morning in 2002. He was straight to the point. 'Chic,' he said, 'how would you like to come back to Thistle and coach the youths?' I was taken aback, to be honest. I couldn't get the word 'yes' out quick enough. I was returning to Firhill which, to many fans, was my spiritual home. I enjoyed the new role and even turned out on two occasions for the first team at the age of thirty-nine.

Somehow it seemed only right and proper that I would end

my playing days at Firhill. Ironically, I played my last senior game against Hibs at Easter Road. My first reserve game for St Mirren two decades beforehand had been at the same ground and, would you believe, my first team debut for the Paisley side was also at Easter Road. Spooky or what?

6

SEEING RED

Willie Young was never in any danger of becoming my favourite referee. I don't think there was ever a chance of me becoming his favourite footballer, either. Well, he did manage to send me off four times during my career. He probably missed the opportunity to flash the red card on at least another four occasions! Too late now, Willie.

I can recall an amusing incident when I was playing for Hibs and my daughter Danielle was the club's mascot before a game against Celtic. Willie was the match official and, of course, there was the usual posing for photographs before the kick-off. My little girl tugged his arm, looked up at him and said, 'Mr Referee, can you do me a favour please?' Taken slightly aback, Willie replied, 'Of course, dear. What do you want me to do for you?' My daughter asked with all the innocence of a five year old, 'Will you not send off my dad today?' Willie was puzzled and replied, 'Who is your dad?' My daughter pointed to me and said, 'That's him there.' Willie thought for a moment, shook his head and answered solemnly, 'Sorry, dear, I can't make that promise!' Willie proved he had a conscience, though, because he only booked me that day.

I got it into my head that Willie Young was out to get me at every opportunity. I have to admit, though, that I did make it easy for him on occasion. I thought I would get my revenge some day if I ever encountered him away from the football field. I'm not talking about anything serious, possibly just a dull one when no-one was looking. Then, one day, I was walking through George Square in Glasgow when, lo and behold, who do I spy coming towards me but my arch enemy. I knew Willie was a lawyer and he was with what I presumed to be a business associate. For a split-second I thought about exacting some retribution for what I had been put through as a player.

As Willie got closer I kept him fixed in my gaze. It could have been a scene from High Noon. I kept walking in his direction and then he looked up and recognised me. 'This is it, Chic,' I thought to myself. 'This is your chance.' Then I was startled when this guy who had banished me four times from games smiled and offered me his hand. I couldn't stop myself. I put out my hand, we shook and I said something like, 'Hi, Willie, how are you doing?' It was all very pleasant and civilized and absolutely no aggro. It wasn't quite the way I had worked out the scenario in my head. Thank goodness.

By the way, Willie has since admitted he thought I was a fair player. I read a piece in a newspaper where he was quoted saying something like, 'Chic Charnley had a lot of skill and was the possessor of a sweet left foot. But, unfortunately, I think he was wired to the moon.' I thought about taking him to court, but, after a bit of consideration, I decided not to. There was every possibility he would have won!

Okay, how come I was ordered off so many times in my career? I reckon it's because I kept getting caught! There were other players out there who could put it about, but they were a bit cleverer than me the way they did it. Where I came from in Possil you took it personally if someone hit you. There was only one answer – reply in kind. Unfortunately, I took that thought onto the park with me on matchday and, of course, that sort of outlook will only get you into trouble. You are playing in a contact sport, after all, and you will be kicked at some point. No player ever went through ninety minutes of a physical game without getting some sort of bump.

It didn't help, either, that I was hyper. I couldn't wait for the game to start when I was in the dressing room. I was raring to go hours before the kick-off. I couldn't wait to get out there and get into the action. Most fans must have thought I was the club captain because I was normally first out the tunnel, running at full pelt and desperate for the referee to blow for the start.

I can look back now and realise some players used to wind me up. Sadly, it was part of my character that I would fall for it all the time. If they kicked me, they knew they would get it back – normally when the match official was watching. I wasn't sly enough, to be honest. I would get my retribution when everyone in the ground was looking on. Well, almost all the time. I remember an incident with Darren Jackson when he was at Dundee United and I was at St Mirren. Darren could be an awkward player, all arms and legs, and he caught me with an elbow in a match at Love Street. Once again, I took it personally. Unfortunately for my opponent his actions came just before the interval. If he had done it ten or fifteen minutes into the game I would have got him back on the field. However, the referee was about to blow for the interval and I wouldn't have the opportunity to return the favour during the time that was left.

I had a full head of steam and was convinced Darren had 'done' me on purpose. I didn't like the idea of being someone else's punchbag. He wasn't going to get away with it. I ran down the tunnel and knew there was an area where the visiting players would have to pass to get to the away team's dressing room. I waited for my chance as Darren, completely unaware of what was around the corner, walked past me. I didn't hesitate. I cracked him on the jaw. Unfortunately for me, my manager Davie Hay

31

and Dundee United boss Jim McLean were right behind Darren and they witnessed the entire scene. Jim lunged at me and Davie pulled him back. The next minute there was a rammy with both managers getting involved. Not the brightest moment for me.

There is a funny postscript to all of this because Jim Duffy signed me for Hibs in January 1997 from Dundee and, coincidentally, Darren had also joined the Edinburgh outfit from United a few years before. I turned up for training on my first day as a Hibs player and I was aware that wherever I was on the pitch, my old adversary was as far away from me as possible. The lad had a good memory. At the end of the session I went over to him and Darren's face was a picture. Clearly, he didn't know what to expect. I put out my hand and said, 'Shake, mate. No hard feelings.' And that was the end of it.

There have been other occasions when I have been deeply embarrassed by some things I have done on a pitch. I still flinch when I bump into former players I have had an encounter with during a game. Some accept that what goes on in a match is all part and parcel of the sport. Others, and I don't blame them one bit, don't think along those lines. I can still recall a game when I was playing for St Mirren against Raith Rovers at Love Street. My boot caught Jimmy Nicholl on the head and I swear it was an accident. I might have been perceived as a bit of a wild man on the pitch but I would never deliberately set out to injure anyone or put them in hospital. Aye, there were a few tasty challenges but nothing malicious. Maybe if it had been anyone else, Jimmy might have accepted the explanation. But he didn't agree with my version and I admit, although on this occasion I am innocent, I still get embarrassed about that incident.

Then there was the time I turned out for a Scotland veterans line-up against England at Hull City's ground. There was the usual banter between the sides before the kick-off and you knew these guys were taking it all very seriously – we were representing our countries, after all. As ever, I got stuck in and, unfortunately, my elbow caught a bloke called John Beresford, who used to play for Newcastle United, smack in the face. Again, it was an accident. It was something I couldn't have done if I tried. Beresford was far from happy, though. I tried to apologise, but he was having none of it. He was convinced I had done it on purpose. At the end of the game I sought him out in the home dressing room. I offered to shake hands, but I was told to eff off. Fair enough. Some guys can take it and others can't. You'll find a lot of players who can dish it out, but they don't want to know when they are on the receiving end.

I accepted that Beresford wasn't going to accept an apology and I left it at that. A doctor had a look at the damage and found that the Englishman had a broken nose. That didn't help matters, trust me. I tried once again to give him an explanation, but, again, I was told to get lost. A couple of days later I received a phone call from a friend informing me that Beresford wanted my telephone number. 'What for?' I enquired. 'He's going to sue you,' I was informed. 'Tell HIM to fuck off,' I replied and, as far as I am aware, that's exactly what he did. I never heard from him again.

I completely lost the plot when I was playing for Clydebank against Morton at Cappielow on Saturday, 27 August 1988 and, once again, I am not proud to look back on my behaviour. Brian Wright was playing for us that afternoon and was up against a bloke called John Boag who was a real tough guy. Poor Brian was carried off after being smashed in the face following a fierce assault from Boag. Brian lost four teeth in the collision and was out of it as he was stretchered off, blood gushing everywhere. Jim Fallon was our coach at the time and he had an assistant called Tony Gervaise. I was still upset at the sight of my big mate in such distress as he left the pitch. I could hardly believe my ears when Gervaise told the players at half time, 'See that attitude shown by Boag? That's the sort of attitude we should be showing.' I couldn't get the thought of my poor team-mate being walloped and carried off out of my head. Gervaise added, 'Are you going to show me that attitude?' I immediately jumped to my feet and said, 'Like this?' And then I punched him smack in the mouth. Understandably, I never played for the Bankies again. The club also parted company with Gervaise, as they looked at both sides of the argument, but he was reinstated shortly afterwards.

Clydebank chairman Jack Steadman must have known what to expect from me. He came to see me playing for Pollok Juniors and I clashed with former Morton right-back Davie Hayes, who was a typical hard-as-nails defender. I sorted him out and, in doing so, earned myself a swift removal from the action. I was surprised when Steadman asked me to come along as a trialist for the Bankies in a reserve fixture against Ayr United at Somerset Park the following Wednesday. He showed a lot of trust in me and offered me signing-on terms after the game. That was surprising, too, because I'd been sent off again. Well, at least he couldn't say I wasn't committed. Mind you, there are some out there who say I should be!

The Bankies gaffer offered me £1,100 to sign there and then. I held out and eventually got £4,000. That was a bit more than he valued me when I played for the Bankies against Rangers in a Testimonial Match for our long-serving goalkeeper Jim Gallacher. The Ibrox side had just paid £1million to Everton for England international right-back Gary Stevens – a lot of money back then. I was in the mood for a wee bit of mischief and as Stevens went to tackle me I neatly stuck the ball through his legs. I ran round him, looked at Jack and said, 'If he's worth a million quid, what does that make me worth?' The Bankies chairman replied, 'Two bob!'

Amazingly, only a week after I left Kilbowie I was playing

against Celtic, of all teams, in the Premier League. Queen of the South, managed by former Rangers winger Davy Wilson, got in touch to offer me terms. They were willing to put £10,000 on the table to play for them on a part-time basis. My mate John Lambie, then in charge of Hamilton Accies, made a counter offer of £2,000 for a full-time contract. Maths not being one of my strong subjects at school, I decided to sign for Accies. So, on 3 September I made my Accies debut against my boyhood heroes at Douglas Park and I thought we played quite well, despite losing 2-1. Frank McAvennie, my old mucker at St Mirren, scored one of Celtic's goals that afternoon.

My last game for Dundee was at St Johnstone and was hardly memorable. I was ordered off for hitting my own team-mate Robbie Reaside and we eventually lost 7-2. Big Robbie, in my opinion, had sold the first goal and I thought I had bailed him out by hitting the equaliser. But I was still fizzing at our central defender and I let him know in no uncertain fashion. There was a bit of backchat and I couldn't stop myself as I slapped him across the face. The referee saw it and off I went.

I was sitting in the dressing room at half time and I was still fuming. The Dundee manager at the time was John McCormack who had taken over from Jim Duffy when he left for Hibs. Now I played alongside John – known as Cowboy to everyone – at St Mirren and he knew I had something of a suspect temperament. He came in at half time and tried to calm me down. Easier said than done, unfortunately. Robbie came in and I flew at him. Punches were thrown as Cowboy tried desperately to come between us. It was a real melee and the St Johnstone players next door must have wondered what the hell was going on in our dressing room. Eventually we were pulled apart, but it was an unacceptable incident and all my fault. I didn't turn up for training on Monday and, after a discussion with the manager, it was agreed that I should part company with the club. I've seen Robbie since and I'm glad to report there are no hard feelings.

Jim Duffy didn't take long to get in touch and I was delighted to link up with him again at Hibs. Strange how things work out, eh? But even there I couldn't keep my hands to myself. Stupidly, I got myself booked after another clash with a team-mate. I hadn't been given a yellow card for about two months when we took on Dundee United at Easter Road. I realised any bother could see me suspended for the last three fixtures of the campaign and the play-offs. Naturally, I didn't want to miss out and I was fortunate enough to give us the lead with a penalty-kick. Then came the inevitable. I had a shouting match with our central defender Joe McLaughlin. Without thinking, I pushed him and, in an instant, knew I would be booked. Sure enough, out came the card and that meant me missing the end of the season.

I calmed down and apologised to McLaughlin at half-time, but I would have quite happily given him a good belt in the kisser. We won 2-0 with another goal from Pat McGinlay but I sat out the games against Kilmarnock (1-1), Celtic (1-3) and Raith Rovers (1-1). At that time there were play-offs between the second bottom team in the Premier League and the runners-up from the First Division. This arrangement only lasted two seasons, but it was a nerve-shredding time for the club and I couldn't do anything to help out. We beat Airdrie 1-0 at Easter Road in the first leg with an own goal from Steve Cooper. Then it was onto dangerous territory for the return at the Shyberry. This time we triumphed 4-2 with goals from Darren Jackson (2), Paul Tosh and Keith Wright.

There is another significant point about the booking against Dundee United. If I had been yellow-carded in any of the remaining games I would have automatically missed the first match of the 1997/98 season. That encounter would have been against Celtic. I played and scored the winning goal in a 2-1 victory!

Another team-mate to incur my wrath was Gardner Spiers at St Mirren. The Paisley side were due to play Dutch aces Feyenoord in the UEFA Cup opening round in season 1983/84. I was just a youngster and the thought of lining up against the likes of Johan Cruyff and Ruud Gullit had tantalising appeal. We lost 1-0 in the first leg at Love Street and I was desperate just to be in the party for the return in Rotterdam. A couple of days before the midweek encounter, there was a list on the notice board of the players who would be making the trip. Imagine my joy when I saw my name in the travelling squad. As usual, though, I found the self-destruct button during training that morning.

Spiers kicked me during a practice match and the red mist came down at an alarming rate. I stepped forward and belted him. It was a perfect connection on his chin. Mike Tyson would have been proud of that effort. Spiers went out like a light. I knocked him cold. My concerned team-mates ran to his aid as I walked away. It was to be an extremely costly punch. When we got back to the ground I looked again at the list of players for the game in Holland. Someone had scratched out my name. I never got anywhere near that plane.

Then there was the time when I was playing in a closed door game for Hamilton against Falkirk. Jim Dempsey was the manager at the time and John McVeigh was an assistant. Although it was just a bounce game, it was becoming a bit tasty. I had words with a Falkirk player and McVeigh, on the touchline, told me to shut up. Once again, my dander was going through the roof, so I simply walked over and punched him. Dempsey wasn't impressed and told me I wouldn't play for Hamilton again. John Lambie had just left the club to go to Partick Thistle and had told me if there was any way he could take me to Firhill he would try to swing it with the board. I think I hastened my departure by walloping the coach. A fee was hastily arranged and I was on my way to the Jags. There is an ironic postscript here because John McVeigh, of all people, also signed me for Thistle in 1998. It took a big man to do that and show there were no hard feelings. To me, John McVeigh is a brilliant bloke.

I was sent off only twice during my four spells at Partick Thistle and that must be some sort of world record for me. However, one of them was totally out of order and even the opponent I was supposed to have kicked tried to dissuade the ref – I think it was John Rowbotham – from showing me the red card. I was playing for Partick Thistle against Aberdeen when I got involved in a tangle with their big, burly frontman Duncan Shearer. We went down, but there was absolutely nothing in it. Unfortunately, the match official didn't see it that way. I saw him walking over, fishing into his top pocket for the red card and I thought, 'Duncan's in trouble.' Genuinely, I believed the ref might have spotted the Dons guy fouling me. I believed it might be a harsh sending-off. I thought it was a lot harsher moments later when the red card was flashed in my direction. I couldn't believe it. I was speechless. To be fair, Big Duncan chimed in with, 'Ref, it was a fair challenge. There was no foul.' The match official refused to listen and off I went again. I was sickened.

However, I've got to laugh at a memory from a few years ago when I got the opportunity to belt a Rangers player and not get into trouble. In fact, I got a round of applause. Let me hastily explain before you get the wrong idea. I was invited to take part in charity boxing event at The Radisson Hotel in Glasgow's city centre. I was told I would be fighting former Ibrox player John McDonald. Would I be interested? Try stopping me! The main event was between Gordon Smith, now the SFA Chief Executive, and politician Tommy Sheridan. It was all for a good cause and I thought it would be a little bit of fun.

Before the fight, John came into the dressing room and said, 'Chic, let's just take it easy. We don't need to punch the hell out of each other. We can get through this with little jabs.' I thought,

'Fair enough.' There were about 1,000 fans crammed into the hotel that evening for the event. My former Thistle team-mate Brian Gallagher and a pal called Sean Sweeney were at the ringside and were yelling, 'Come on the Fighting Irish' as I stepped into the ring. I winked over at John and he returned the compliment. Then what happened? The wee bugger caught me with a punch. Now that was a mistake, believe me. I walloped him all over the place and must have knocked him out about six times!

It wasn't the first time I had clashed with the Rangers player. My last game for Ayr United was a reserve fixture against Rangers at Ibrox. I recall there were about 2,000 at the game and, as you might have anticipated, I was desperate to do well against Celtic's age-old rivals. I was getting in about it and the Rangers supporters were giving me the treatment. I lapped it up. Then I caught McDonald with a sore one. It was a hard challenge, but the referee was far from impressed. He ran over, pointed to the tunnel and said, 'Off!' The home support were cheering big-style as I made my way to the dressing room. I flicked a V-sign at them and, just to annoy them further, I started to bless myself! They were screaming their heads off and the police actually came onto the pitch to grab me and huckle me down the tunnel. I thought I was going to be arrested. Thankfully, they didn't pursue the matter, but my Ayr United gaffers were swift to tell me shortly afterwards that they were scrapping my contract.

I was also red-carded playing for St Mirren in a Scottish Cup replay against Hearts at Tynecastle. We had drawn in the first game and were right up for the second match in midweek. As can so often happen, there are little feuds from the first game that can carry on into another encounter coming up so quickly against the same opposition. Kenny McDowall, now first team coach at Rangers, and I came up with a little scheme that might fox the referee. If I was kicked by someone, Kenny would exact retribution. I agreed to do the same for him. Sometimes it is too obvious that a player is hunting down someone who has thumped him and the referee is well aware of it. Alas, it didn't work quite as planned. I booted someone, the ref, as ever, was in the vicinity and off I went. It didn't take long before Kenny saw red, too, and joined me in the dressing room. Maybe not our best plan.

Another game that got more than a little out of hand was a St Mirren match against Ayr United at Somerset Park. Well, a little out of hand might just be a bit of an understatement – we ended up with only eight players on the field at time-up. I was ordered off and so, too, were my colleagues Paul Lambert and Barry Lavety. Paul was as tough as anyone and I remember a training session at Love Street where we were in opposition and going at each other hammer and tongs. Davie Hay shouted from the touchline, 'Hey, you two, cut it out. You're supposed to be my midfield ball-players.'

Training sessions at Love Street could be fairly ferocious and there was another incident when Guni Torfasson, our Icelandic player, was getting involved with another player. They were kicking the shit out of each other and once more the boss intervened. He shouted, 'If you guys want to fight why don't you go behind one of the goals and have a scrap?' Peace broke out immediately.

I must have made some sort of history when I was booked during a penalty-kick shoot-out. Okay, how on earth did that happen? Easy when you're me. A Cup-tie against Dunfermline had ended all-square after extra time and went to a spot-kick showdown. The Fifers had a keeper called Andy Rhodes at the time and he was a bit brash. He was doing his level best to put off the St Mirren players as they prepared to take their kick. I stepped up to place the ball on the spot when I heard, 'Hey, Charnley, you've no chance. Don't even bother taking the kick – you're a cert to miss.' He kept it up all the way as I prepared to hit the ball. Whack! Goal! I followed the ball into the net and said something not too complimentary to the beaten keeper. Alas, it was within the hearing distance of the whistler who immediately produced a yellow card.

Since quitting playing I have done some after-dinner speaking and I've bumped – not literally – into a few former referees who are also on the circuit. I recall an incident when I was on the same list as John Rowbotham, the match official who hailed from Kirkcaldy and who, I am fairly certain, was the bloke who sent me off for nothing in that match against Aberdeen. He was telling the story about a player who kept swearing at him, but the ref could do nothing as the lad claimed he had Tourettes. You know that affliction that means an individual is unable to control his language on occasion. If only I had thought of that one when I was playing – it might have cut down my red and yellow cards fairly dramatically!

I'm glad to say there were a handful of match officials I didn't get on the wrong side of. Bob Tait, for a start. Goodness knows how many games he refereed when I was playing yet I believe he didn't book me even once. There are some match officials who can tell a foul from a good, hard challenge. There are others, unfortunately, who can't. I'm not too sure how highly Tait rated me. There was an incident in a game at Easter Road when someone threw a ten pence piece at the ref. Unflinchingly, Tait picked up the coin, handed it to me and said, 'There you are, Chic, that's all your worth.' Thanks, mate! Brian McGinlay was another official I liked and he never booked me, either.

If only there had been a few more refs around like Bob and Brian – I would probably have played about another hundred more games in my career!

However, as I said earlier, I still feel a deep embarrassment about some things that happened out on the pitch in the heat of the moment. I was always highly charged and there was nothing anyone could do to change my character. I never went out looking for trouble, but, honestly, there were occasions it came seeking me. There was nothing left to do but confront it. But there is a lot to look back on with a bit of regret. Unfortunately, opponents seemed to know how to trigger me off. On too many occasions, I didn't let them down.

7

THE DREAM THAT DIED

There's only one person to blame for Chic Charnley never real-ising his boyhood dream of signing for Celtic. Me. It was my lifelong ambition to play in those world famous green-and-white hoops. I managed to do so once and only once. However, it was entirely my own fault that my solitary appearance wasn't followed by any more. I can't point the finger at anyone else. It was all down to me. The opportunity was there and I managed to blow it big-style.

Lou Macari was the Celtic manager in 1994 when, at the age of thirty-one, I was invited to play for Celtic in a testimonial match against Manchester United at Old Trafford. I received the telephone call from Partick Thistle boss John Lambie and I thought he was pulling my leg. I knew him well enough over the years to realise he was prone to the odd prank or two. There had been no advance warning and, as it was the end of the season, I had gone out with my mates for a few beers. Well, more than a few, as I recall. But the new season was a long way off and I knew a lot of my fellow professionals really let their hair down at the completion of a long, arduous campaign. I was no different.

So, I wasn't in the best of nick when John Lambie made that call. Once he had persuaded me he was not winding me up, I thought, 'Oh God! I can't play in this condition.' The game was the next evening and I was told I had to turn up to get the coach to Manchester with the rest of the Celtic players. There was no way I was getting on that coach. I was certain they would detect I was reeking of booze from the night before. They would have slung me off at Parkhead Cross!

I concocted some sort of story that went along the lines of me making my own way to Old Trafford and catching up with the rest of the team before the game. Celtic accepted my explanation and I breathed a sigh of relief. My mates and I had already arranged to go down to the game anyway, to support Celtic. Now I had the chance of actually playing at Old Trafford. It was unbelievable. I took everything that was possible to get rid of the smell of stale beer. You name it, I drank it, sucked it, sprayed it. I fretted all the way to Manchester in the car with my pals. The only football equipment I had with me were my boots, wrapped in a plastic bag. We made a couple of stops on the way to the game and we passed several Celtic supporters' buses heading for Manchester. My mates were pointing at me and saying, 'See that guy there? He's playing for Celtic tonight.' The fans nodded their heads and replied, 'Aye, so he is!'

When we got to Manchester I had to change in the car to get out of my travelling clothes and get into my best suit. Then I met up with Lou Macari and the Celtic players. I was so proud to be in their company. I wasn't visualising the big picture, though. I couldn't look beyond simply playing in this one game. I didn't fully appreciate that I was being handed the opportunity of a lifetime to realise my dream. It was a testimonial and I assumed it was a one-off occasion. However, I did realise that Lou Macari rated me to a certain extent. But I thought it was a gesture by Celtic because I had never hidden my passion for the club. It was well known where my affections lay – just ask any Rangers fan! No matter who I was playing for, they always gave me stick. To be fair, I wound them up at every opportunity, too. All good fun!

I boarded the coach with the rest of my new team-mates and I am not afraid to admit that my eyes filled up as we made our way through the thousands of Celtic supporters on our way to Old Trafford. Me? Crying like a baby? Given my so-called reputation that may be difficult to imagine, maybe, but it's the truth nevertheless. Eventually the players were escorted to the away dressing room and the moment I had waited for all my life was only minutes away – I was about to pull that coveted hooped shirt over my head. My chest was pumping up and my heart was beating like never before. I was going to play for Celtic and I was going to enjoy every minute of it. And I did.

As we kicked the ball about in the warm-up I looked up the vast stands of Manchester United's superb stadium and all I could see were green-and-white scarves everywhere. This was a Testimonial Match for United's Mark Hughes, but there seemed to be more Celtic fans in the ground than their United counterparts. It was a truly amazing experience. Awesome and unforgettable. Suddenly I was aware the Celtic support were chanting, 'One Chic Charnley . . . there's only one Chic Charnley.' To be absolutely honest, I was so overcome I started to cry. I couldn't prevent the tears from streaming down my face. Those wonderful fans had just taken me to a place I could only dream about. Lou Macari was so concerned about my welfare and ability to carry on that he sent on Frank Connor, one of his assistants, to see if I was okay. 'Chic, can you play?' asked Frank. 'Just try and stop me,' I answered. This was the biggest moment in my entire career and I wasn't going to miss out. I reassured him I would be fine. I have a tape of the supporters chanting my name and I still feel as emotional today as I did all those years ago.

What a night it became as Celtic won 3-1 and I set up one of the goals for Simon Donnelly with a through pass into his tracks and he stuck it away with a fair amount of style. As I recall, he scored two that evening. My son Gary had asked me before the game to get Ryan Giggs's autograph as he was a big fan of the Welsh ace. His request popped into my head with about ten minutes to go and I went over to Ryan to ask him if he would exchange shirts with me at the end. He very kindly agreed and, sure enough, we traded our jerseys on the pitch at full-time. However, there is always a snag with me. I didn't want to part with my Celtic shirt because it meant so much to me. I made my way to the United dressing room afterwards, explained the situation to Ryan and, thankfully, he returned the jersey.

There's a photograph of me running away from Eric Cantona with a broad smile on my face that evening and I've been asked countless times what I was laughing at. Eric, a genuine world famous superstar, had tried to play the ball through my legs, a nutmeg as it's known in football. I wasn't having any of that. I snapped my legs shut, got the ball under control and swerved past the Frenchman. I looked at the Celtic dug-out and caught the eye of Brian Scott, the club's physiotherapist. 'Who does he think he is?' I said and the Celtic bench dissolved into laughter. It was a magic moment and I was so happy that a snapper had caught the image perfectly. A friend of mine is a bit of an artist and he painted the picture for me. It hangs proudly on a wall at home, a constant reminder of the night I played for Celtic.

I was still bubbling with enthusiasm and emotion afterwards when Lou Macari pulled me aside and asked me if I wanted to go on tour with Celtic. They were due to head out for a three-week trip to Canada and North America. It was yet another occasion for me to demonstrate so capably that I have the unerring ability to make the wrong decision. Looking back, of course, I should have leapt at the invitation. There should have been no hesitation whatsoever. But, as ever, there was a problem. Partick Thistle had organised a week's end-of-season holiday for the players in the Algarve. I would have had to miss out to go with Celtic. Really, there was no decision to make, was there? I should have binned the seven-day jolly in Portugal to take the chance to show Lou Macari he should make me a permanent fixture in his first team squad. So, what did I do? I went with the Thistle lads, of course. To be honest, I don't think Lou actually wanted to sign me. He thought I could play a bit, but did he really want me? Deep down, that was the impression I had.

The Celtic manager didn't push me to go with them. He didn't attempt to persuade me it would be better for my career if I travelled with the club. If he had told me that any chance of joining Celtic would end there and then if I didn't agree to travel with them there would have been no alternative. I would have been waiting for the rest of the squad at the airport on the day of departure. I would have been there a day early. I was still on a high at Old Trafford and probably wasn't thinking straight but if Lou Macari had been more forceful I would have been on the flight with the rest of the Celtic lads. Although, as I've said, I didn't think Lou Macari really wanted me that badly. Having said that, I still believed there would be some sort of offer made to me when Celtic came home. In fact, Lou Macari, despite my impressions, said as much and I know I don't have defective hearing. Off I went to the Algarve with my Firhill buddies and wondered what lay ahead for yours truly during the summer break. I could hardly take my mind off the thought of finally signing for Celtic.

Lou Macari never did get back to me and I heard afterwards from a sports journalist friend that he had said something along the lines of, 'If Chic Charnley really wanted to be a Celtic player he should have been on the trip.' If only the Celtic manager had said those words to me in Manchester. I have to say that I was hurt when I heard this. However, as I said right at the start, I blame no-one but myself. It was an opportunity spectacularly spurned and I never got the call to play in those hoops again. I have absolutely no doubt, though, that Lou Macari played a part in my decision-making at Old Trafford. If he had laid everything on the line I would have been packing my travelling gear seconds after getting home.

Ironically, I wouldn't have played for Macari anyway, because he was sacked during the summer after a fall-out with the club's owner Fergus McCann. Tommy Burns, of course, took over and I might just have been his sort of player. Tommy, a true Celtic legend who lost his gallant battle against cancer in 2008, was an elegant left-sided midfielder during his glorious playing days. I know he appreciated my style of play.

Tommy actually once tried to sign me for Kilmarnock when I came back from my stint in Sweden with Djurgardens in 1993. I was thirty at the time and had already had talks with John Lambie and chairman Jim Oliver at Partick Thistle just before Tommy came in. I was in a sweat. I really fancied playing for such a great sportsman and wonderful gentleman as Tommy at Rugby Park, but I had given my word to John and Jim I would accept their offer. I couldn't go back on that and, unfortunately, I had to tell Tommy. He fully understood and wished me the best of luck. How ironic is football, though? I signed on the Friday for Thistle and made my second debut for them the following day at Firhill against Killie, of all clubs. I also managed to set up the winning goal. Unfortunately, it was for Killie! I passed the ball straight to their striker Danny Crainie and he whacked an effort into the back of our net. I heard John Lambie mutter in that gravel voice of his, 'We should have let the hopeless bastard sign for Kilmarnock!'

History now tells you I never did get the chance to play for Tommy Burns. A year after turning out at Old Trafford I might have been performing in the Scottish Cup Final in the hoops against Airdrie at Hampden in the showpiece game at the end of the season. It's a heartwarming thought, but the reality of the situation was vastly different. Instead, I was out of work, freed by Partick Thistle. A sports reporter telephoned me to ask how I felt about the situation. I felt like crying.

I don't think Liam Brady fancied me, either. Well, his missus certainly didn't. John Lambie and Gerry Collins went to the World Cup Finals in America in 1994 and were sitting in the stand beside Brady and his wife watching one of the games. Somehow the conversation came round to yours truly when Mrs Brady chimed in with, 'Chic Charnley? He's just a pub team player.' John Lambie, quick as a flash, replied, 'If your man had eleven pub team players like Chic Charnley he might still be Celtic manager today!' Thanks, John.

Celtic, of course, remain special to me, the club I adored and supported as a boy. I'm still a season-ticket holder at Parkhead to this day. And, yes, I often wonder what might have happened if I had taken an attack of brains that May evening at Old Trafford back in 1994 and Lou Macari had spelled out everything clearly. I remember once saying to Billy McNeill, who was the Celtic boss at the time, 'Why have you never signed me?' Billy didn't even blink as he replied, 'Chic, son, I like to sleep at night!' However, there was one evening when we were both at a function and Billy told me, 'You know, Chic, my right hand tells me to sign you and the left hand says no.' Unfortunately, the left hand won, but the Celtic manager, like everyone else, knew I would have done anything to sign for that club.

When Billy McNeill went through his quadruple heart bypass in the mid-nineties I sent him a message, saying, 'You could have had that operation years ago if you had signed me.' I hope he saw the funny side.

8

BLADE RUNNER IN MARYHILL

I sensed danger. The guy appeared more than just a bit irate and was certainly looking for trouble. The clue, I suppose, was the Samurai sword he was wielding rather crazily above his head. I have to admit this was not a typical day at training for Partick Thistle's professional footballers.

I was in my second stint as a Firhill player and, as usual, we changed into our training gear before heading off for a session at nearby Ruchill Park. On this morning, though, a couple of yobs thought it would be a good idea to dish out some stick to the players. 'Hey, Charnley, you're fuckin' useless,' came the witty riposte from one of them. They picked on a few of my team-mates, too. We were ignoring these two wastes of oxygen and thought they would get fed up and go off and annoy someone or something else. We were wrong. These nyaffs were at full throttle and they kept up a barrage of abuse for ages. Eventually, I lost my temper. I shouted over at them, 'Why don't you come back in about an hour's time when we've finished training and we can have a wee discussion?'

To my surprise, Tweedledumb and Tweedledumber took off. I didn't think any more of it as we continued to work on our fitness levels. About an hour later I heard a voice shouting out, 'Charnley, we're ready for our discussion.' I looked round and, sure enough, our pair of hecklers had returned. This time, though, they looked as though they wanted to do more than have a natter. For a start, one of them was carrying a huge sabre. It wasn't an ordinary-looking sword you see in the Zorro movies, but one of those curved Japanese-type weapons that would terrify the life out of you. His pal was a bit more conservative, he was just carrying a carving knife. They had also acquired an angry-looking dog from somewhere. These guys were ready for business.

I had my back to them when they returned. One of my team-mates said, 'Chic, look behind you.' My first expression was, 'Oh, shit!' The two thugs looked as though they might want a few Partick Thistle scalps before they moved on. After gulping in some fresh air, I monitored the unsavoury situation. Some of my Thistle colleagues were in the same frame of mind as myself – this pair could do with a good hiding. Others decided it would be best to get back to the stadium as swiftly as possible. You just knew, though, that these halfwits would be back the following day once again noising us up and going through the same boring routine. Gerry Collins and Gordon Rae were two strapping six-footers who were afraid of no-one on the football pitch. Or off it, for that matter. I knew they could handle themselves. The three of us faced up to the sabre-carrying lout, his mate with the knife and the growling mutt.

There was nothing left for it, but to go at them. We started to run in their direction and, amazingly, the first thing to scarper was the dog! It took off down the hill as fast as its legs could take it. Smart dog. As I raced towards the moron with the Samurai I picked up a traffic cone. It didn't look like a fair fight, but there wasn't anything else handy. Sadly, no-one had left a spare machete lying around the public park that day. Gerry and Gordon made a beeline for the guy with the knife. I kept on charging towards the other bloke and, out the corner of my eye, I saw my two mates jump on top of his pal. My adversary looked at the mess

51

Gerry and Gordon were making of the knifeman and suddenly turned and chased after the pooch. At that point, I realise I should have stopped my pursuit of this headcase. That would have been the bright thing to do. So I kept running after him.

I was waving the traffic cone above my head and was startled when he stopped abruptly and, as I got closer, swung the sabre at me. I instinctively put out my hand and I felt the blade slash through my palm. I was raging, to say the least, and I dropped the traffic cone. I wasn't going to back out, though. I whacked him with a right-hander and down he went in a heap, thankfully releasing his weapon as he did so. We were now on a level footing, both unarmed. I won't go into the gory detail, but, suffice to say, we never saw those guys again when we were training. And God only knows where the dog went!

My hand had to be bandaged – I'm still scarred to this day – and I was visiting Margaret, who was in for a check-up, in hospital later that evening. She took one look at my damaged hand and said, 'How did that happen?' I didn't want to worry her needlessly, so I told a small fib. 'Oh, it's nothing,' I said. 'Just a training ground accident.' She looked at me and said, 'No, it's not – you've been on the news! Can I not leave you for a couple of hours without you getting into trouble?' I was innocent, but I was still getting a telling-off!

I thought I might have a reasonable claim for criminal damages, so off I went to see a lawyer. I'll always remember his expression. He said, 'It's a penalty kick. You can't fail.' Oh, yes I could. I was asked to go along to the Maryhill Police Station where the CID had arranged for a line-up. There were about five guys facing me and, sure enough, I recognised the two offenders. 'Just point out the characters you saw that day, Mr Charnley,' said one officer. Now where I come from in Possil you never grassed on anyone. You simply took care of business in the way you saw fit. I couldn't become a snitch.

I looked at the guys and said, 'It might have been number two. Or it might have been number four. I'm not sure.' I could see the local bobbies were far from impressed by my powers of observation. Or lack of them, as the case may be. I couldn't find it within myself to finger the two buffoons. Eventually, the cops got more than a little frustrated and slung me out of the police station. John Lambie was with me and he tried to explain why I hadn't named names. They threw him out, too!

The police followed up by telling me I wouldn't get any compensation because I shouldn't have chased the would-be musketeer down the hill in the first place. And just to rub it in I got a bill for £150 from my lawyer.

Thankfully, that Samurai incident was never repeated, but it is still my genuine belief that some football fans go over the top in their criticism of players. OK, they pay their hard-earned cash to get into the ground on matchday and they insist they have the right to say what they want – free speech and all that. It has to be admitted that a lot of their comments are hardly constructive. Some of their 'advice' is not legal or physically possible! I've been around the block more than most people and a lot of comments from the terracings or stands never upset me. A lot of what they come out with is supposed to be humorous, but most of it is as funny as an ingrowing toenail. There was one bloke, though, who did get to me one day when I was playing for Partick Thistle against Falkirk at their old Brockville stadium. This guy focused completely on me. I think he started his criticism at the warm-up and just kept up a steady stream of four-letter words throughout the first-half. I looked at him as I made my way towards the tunnel at the interval. I made sure I knew where he was standing in the crowd.

As I came out for the second-half, the abuse kicked in immediately. 'Hey, Charnley,' he said. 'Call yourself a footballer? You couldn't pass water.' As it happens, I wasn't having a particularly good afternoon and he was right, my passing wasn't up to scratch. It wasn't down to this guy having a go at me – I was just having a stinker. Ten minutes or so into the half, the ball went out for a shy just in front of my abuser. I ran over to take it and, sure enough, I heard the words, 'Charnley, you're fuckin' crap.' Now I've admitted I could hardly hit the target that day, but I couldn't possibly miss this loudmouth. As I motioned to pick up the ball for the throw-in, I simply hammered it in his direction. Bingo! It was a direct hit. The ball thudded into his face, I'm sure I saw a pair of false teeth take off into orbit and the bloke collapsed backwards. He recovered, but, remarkably, I didn't hear another word from him for the rest of the game.

9

PLAYING IN PARADISE

You get asked a lot of daft questions in football. Some are as dopey as asking the late American president's wife, 'Apart from that, Mrs Lincoln, what did you think of the play?' Folk often enquire what it was it like to perform at Celtic Park. What do you think? It's an unbelievable experience and, of course, would have been even more memorable if I had been wearing green and white hoops. As I prepared for my first game against my boyhood idols I wasn't too sure how I would react. I was a Hamilton Accies player and, as a professional, I knew I would do my utmost for them. However, it was a very strange feeling lining up against Celtic on that initial occasion.

I was basically going about my game when suddenly I was sent hurtling through the air. I thought I had been hit by a train. I looked up and there was the powerful figure of Roy Aitken looming menacingly over me. I had been hammered from behind by Crocodile Ardossan. All bets were off after that. I got stuck in and gave as good as I got. Anyone witnessing that encounter would have found it extremely hard to believe Celtic were the club closest to my heart. I threw myself into challenges, fought for everything, ran around all day and was pinging passes all over park. That's the way it should have been, of course. Big Roy did me a favour that day by battering into me. You could say it was a real wake-up call.

Actually, Roy and I became team-mates at St Mirren in 1992 when Davie Hay bought him from Newcastle United. I will state here and now that the man known as 'The Bear' was the most complete professional I have played alongside – and that's saying something when you consider the number of players I lined up with during my career. He didn't have anything to prove to anyone, of course. He had been there, seen it, done it and had the T-shirt at club and country level. Big Roy had captained Celtic and Scotland and had been idolised by the Parkhead support. He may have been in the twilight of his career when he joined St Mirren, but if that was him winding down then God only knows what he was like when he was in his prime and had ambitions to achieve.

He was a great spirit and presence in the dressing room and had genuine leadership qualities. It was impossible to keep up with him in training. He was a massive guy with muscles on his muscles. I still shudder when I think back to the clattering dunts he dished out. I liked Roy and it was a pleasure to be his team-mate for a while. If only it had been as a Celtic player.

There was an occasion in training with St Mirren when Roy, never one to hold back, caught me on the knee and I felt pain shooting through my body. 'I'm not letting you away with that, mate,' I thought to myself. The next opportunity I got I went in hard on Roy. It had all the desired effect of a moth charging at a bull. I think I bounced about six yards off him and he hardly even noticed. I didn't bother trying that again.

Naturally enough, a lot of my friends are Celtic supporters and they used to give me pelters when I was due to play against them. 'Remember, Chic, no tackling the lads,' they would say. 'None of this passing the ball stuff.' It was all good-natured banter because they knew I would give my all for the club that was paying my wages. I recall a game at Celtic Park when I was playing for Partick Thistle and we were getting a succession of corner-kicks on the right. I was swinging them in on top of the goalkeeper with my left foot. They were all fairly accurate, I'm delighted to say, and they were creating all sorts of confusion. The Celtic support seemed more than a little anxious. I think it was goalless at the time, midway through the second-half. I just kept piling them under the crossbar. As I ran to take another I heard this voice say, 'Hey, Charnley, you're supposed to be one of us!' As I recall we got a 1-1 draw that afternoon and I set up the equaliser for Tom Smith.

Of course, I'm the guy who wrecked Henrik Larsson's debut for Celtic. It was the opening day of the 1997/98 season and the Parkhead outfit had undergone a massive facelift. Wim Jansen had replaced the unfortunate Tommy Burns, who never got the success his ambitious ideals deserved, and the Dutchman had brought in new players, Henrik among them. The game was at Easter Road and I can tell you that Jim Duffy, the Hibs gaffer, had us well up for it. 'Let's get off to a great start,' he urged his players. 'A win here will set us up nicely.'

We opened the scoring through Lee Power, but Celtic equalised with a header from their centre-half Malky Mackay. The game ebbed and flowed in the second-half and that was when Wim Jansen decided to introduce Henrik Larsson to Scottish football. He sent on the Swede as a substitute and I couldn't thank him enough for that decision. Henrik was pinned back in a defensive position on Celtic's left when he tried to clear his lines. He fluffed his kick completely and sent the ball rolling in my direction. I was running in, completely unmarked, and could hardly believe my good fortune. The ball was perfectly weighted, too, as it ran towards my left peg. Without any hesitation, I smacked it first time from about twenty-five yards and my effort took off like an Exocet missile. Celtic goalkeeper Gordon Marshall hadn't a chance. No-one on the planet could have kept that shot out of the net, even if I do say so myself.

It was the perfect strike and, as luck would have it, was the winning goal. I celebrated big-style and John Hughes actually pushed me into the crowd. Then I ran over to the Celtic dug-out and caught the eye of Murdo MacLeod, who had been my manager at Dumbarton for about five minutes. He had just been named Jansen's assistant and I shouted at Murdo, 'Tell him to sign me!' Jansen must have wondered what on earth was going on. Hibs actually did get off to a flying start that season, but things were to change dramatically as the campaign and the drama unfolded. We were top of the league for a spell and playing some fine stuff. I was getting rave reviews and, remarkably, there was even a call from some quarters for me to get a call-up for Scotland. Dreams in football swiftly become nightmares, though. Hibs went into freefall, hit rock-bottom and, as so often happens, the directors took the inevitable action – they sacked Jim Duffy and his assistant Jackie McNamara. They brought in Alex McLeish from Motherwell and I realised only too quickly that my days at Easter Road were numbered.

I knew McLeish didn't fancy me. I recall playing for Dundee in a reserve game when he was player/manager at Well. He saw me and said, 'You're just like a bad penny, aren't you? You just keep turning up. So, this is where you are playing now?' I didn't appreciate the comment and I realised he didn't think much of me. The board might as well have thrown me out with Duff and Jackie when they brought in McLeish. I don't suppose I helped my case by not bothering to turn up for training on the Monday. I didn't go in on Tuesday, either. Eventually, I went to the club on Wednesday and McLeish was holding talks with the players. There were about thirty-five of us assembled in front of him and McLeish ordered me to go and stand beside some youth players. Afterwards we had a wee chat and he said, 'I think it's best that you move on.' Frankly, I didn't blame him and, to this day, I don't hold it against him.

Before I went, though, I was due a settlement, but I discovered it was £500 short. Needless to say, the club didn't want to stump up. Chief Executive Rod Petrie was a tough negotiator and, as they say, every penny was a prisoner. Billy McNeill, my old idol at Celtic, had been brought to the club by Jim Duffy in a backroom capacity. While I was haggling with Petrie, Big Billy came up with a brainwave. 'Why don't we flip a coin?' said the Lisbon legend. Petrie must have thought he had at least a fifty/fifty chance in this scenario and was prepared to take the risk. Billy produced a coin, I called heads and the Celtic icon didn't let me down. I got it right with a little help from Billy and I duly received my money. Actually, it didn't matter if it had come down tails. I wasn't moving until I got my full entitlement, anyway.

So, what had kicked off as looking like being a stupendous season had taken a wicked downturn. I was freed in March and joined Partick Thistle for a third time after playing a one-off trial game for Clydebank. Of course, Hibs were relegated. Celtic and Henrik Larsson? They might have lost their opening two games of the campaign – they were also beaten 2-1 by Dunfermline a week after we defeated them – but went on to win the league title and thwart Rangers' attempt to clinch ten-in-a-row.

I played five games for Thistle before being released at the end of the season. John McVeigh, who was also sacked, took a chance on me by bringing me to Firhill and, in fairness, I think I let him down. He threw me a lifeline and I ignored it. Sorry, John. Henrik Larsson was on his way to iconic status with the Celtic support where he enjoyed seven fabulous years and scored a remarkable 242 goals in 315 games. Me? It was 1998 and, at the age of thirty-five, I had to start again. I was on my way to Tarff Rovers!

10

THE REAL HARD MEN

My old St Mirren team-mate Billy Abercromby was so ferocious I used to keep well away from him in training. Honestly, you thought you were playing for the World Cup the way wee Billy threw himself into tackles. He was impossible to calm down. 'Billy, remember I'm actually your team-mate,' I would say. 'We both play for the same side.' It made little or no difference to Aber as he simply kept flying into one reckless challenge after another. Thank goodness he was on our side on matchday.

Aber, of course, got instant notoriety when he was sent off THREE times in the one game! I know you can only technically be red-carded once, but the referee can add to the punishment as he sees fit and the match official that night was a bloke called Louis Thow who could be a bit fussy. He wasn't impressed by Aber, that's for sure, and he included another two offences that, as far as penalty points were concerned, just about totalled another two orderings-off. I recall Aber going into a challenge in a game against Kilmarnock that left their player Gordon Wylde with a broken leg. There's no way I am saying it was deliberate, but it certainly looked dangerous. I don't think the Killie lad ever played again.

Graeme Souness thought twice about getting into a ruck with Aber on another occasion. My St Mirren team-mate got involved with the Rangers player/manager, a guy who had his own reputation for being more than capable of dishing it out, and there came a flashpoint in their confrontation. Aber actually motioned for Souness to come over with a 'bring it on' gesture. Souness didn't want to know. I don't think he went anywhere near our player again that day. That tells you all you need to know about Aber, I think.

I have to state here and now that I was never intimidated by any opponent. Sure, there were some tough guys out there, but I can say in all honesty that I was afraid of no-one. I can't think of any time when I thought twice about going into a hard challenge with an opponent. It must have had something to do with my good old Possil upbringing! Of course, there are a lot of players who like to be portrayed as hard men in football. They masquerade under this image believing it impresses the fans. Yes, I'm aware that supporters like to see hard tackles and it is a competitive sport, after all. They must have enjoyed the days when I was up against Dave McKinnon, who played for Airdrie and Rangers. Wee Dave and I didn't really need a ball during the action. We made a beeline for each other straight from the kick-off and that was the end of the actual football as far as we were concerned.

We spent most of the ninety minutes punching hell out of each other off the ball. He was a tough cookie, no doubt about it. We both gave as good as we got and at the end of a torrid encounter we limped off and would growl something like, 'See you next time.' I still laugh at the time I met my old mates in a pub in Possil called The Comet, known locally as Hitler's Bunker. Honestly, there are no windows in the place, but I would meet up with old pals such as Pop McAusline and Jimmy Lawrence, among others, for a small aperitif after training. I was at Partick Thistle at the time and would get there at about one o'clock for a wee Salvador Dali – or swally, if you prefer.

I was there with about ten of my pals when I saw this figure furtively look through the door and then decide it was safe enough to come in. It was Dave McKinnon who was a brewery rep at the time. He must have drawn the short straw. Now the guys I was with were more than just a bit tasty. They weren't hanging around waiting for an audition to become the next boyband, that's for sure. I was terrified of them and I knew them all! Dave was standing at the bar and was looking around The Bunker when his eyes picked out me. Honestly, he went as white as Casper the Ghost. There I was sitting with a load of my cronies and he was in deepest, darkest Possil in a pub with no windows. On his own. Without a friend in sight.

The alarm bells in his head must have been going off big-style when I got up from the table and made my way towards him. Honestly, he looked more than just a little startled. After all, we had spent every game kicking the shit out of each other. What was coming next? I tried to keep a straight face as I made my way towards him. I then put out my hand and said, 'Shake, Davie, what brings you around these parts?' His relief was fairly evident, I can tell you. He got out of there faster than any time I had ever seen him run on a pitch. However, it was a funny incident as I'm sure he'd agree now. Years later.

Another bloke who beat a hasty retreat from Hitler's Bunker was my old Thistle boss Sandy Clark. He was asked to smash a bottle full of money for charity and, after discovering what the pub was all about, roped in Brian Gallagher and me as sort of minders. 'You know the place and the guys who drink there,' said Sandy. 'You're coming with me.' He couldn't wait to get out of the place as soon as possible. I liked Sandy and, to be honest, I don't think he got any luck at all in his short time as gaffer at Firhill. I recall a game against Airdrie at Broomfield when we were kicking into a gale and the sun was in our eyes. We went in at the interval and thought at least the weather would be on our side in the second-half. I know this sounds impossible, but I swear it did happen – in the space of ten minutes or so the wind had changed and even the sun, somehow, was back in our eyes.

Sandy could be quite an excitable bloke and there was a day when he was less than satisfied with a first-half performance from his troops. He was raging and aimed a kick at a plastic bin. Unfortunately for him, his foot lodged in the bin and he couldn't shake it off. The more he tried, the more it seemed to stick. He was fuming and his mood wasn't helped by the sight of everyone else in the dressing room cracking up. It was like something out of a Charlie Chaplin movie.

I was carried off only once in my career and that came after a meeting with a bloke called Bobby Thomson, who played for Hamilton Accies. It was my first period at Clydebank and I was still learning the ropes. Now Bobby was a bloke who looked as though he shaved with a blowtorch. He was a big lad, but that didn't deter yours truly when the opportunity was presented to give him a kick. That was a mistake. Bobby, like the old pro he was, didn't react immediately. He bided his time and I was bang on his radar.

Then, when I least expected it, he made his move. He came thundering right through a challenge and just about cut me in two. I went down in a heap and it was game over. There was no way I was going to get back to my feet after that attack. The stretcher was called for and I made my exit with Thomson, no doubt, happy with his day's work. I learned a lesson there and then. Watch your back at all times or suffer the consequences.

I once actually walked off with a broken leg, would you believe? Aye, they breed them tough in Possil. It was the opening day of the 1992/93 season and St Mirren, then managed by Jimmy Bone, were taking on Raith Rovers at Stark's Park in a First Division encounter. As you might expect, I could never wait to get involved and the first game of a brand new campaign used to get me excited. What lay ahead in the months to come? Well, for me, it was a lot of hospital visits, unfortunately. The game was jogging along nicely when I was challenged by Shaun Dennis, a big, hard guy who could put it about. I wasn't complaining, though, because I could always give as good as I got. I felt a twinge, but tried to play through it.

At one stage, though, I realised I wasn't 100 per cent and the best thing to do in those circumstances is to get off the pitch and not put the onus on your team-mates. You can be as brave as you like, but there is little point in the team carrying a passenger, as far as I am concerned. I signalled to Jimmy Bone, 'I'll need to come off.' The pain was excruciating. The boss nodded for me to depart the action. He put on a young lad called Barry Lavety in my place. Our physiotherapist was a young bloke called Andy Binning. I recall he used to take a lot of stick off the Paisley players because his dad was a top cop in the Stirlingshire Police. Andy had a look at my leg and applied the usual ice pack. 'That should do the trick,' he said, rather optimistically I thought. It was painful, but Andy thought it would calm down overnight and I would be OK in the morning. He was the expert so I took his word for it.

In fact, I even went out that Saturday night for a few drinks with my mates. I reckoned it might help deaden the pain of my injury and also the fact Raith had walloped us 7-0! I recall Gordon Dalziel got a hat-trick and Craig Brewster chipped in with two. What a way to start a season. I was having a pint or two with my mates but I had to call it a day early in proceedings when my leg started to throb like hell. I went along to the hospital the following morning and they put me through the X-ray. I was informed I had a hairline fracture! And our physio thought some ice would work miracles. I was told I would be out for about eight weeks and, in fact, I missed thirteen games. I don't think the team missed me because, as I recall, St Mirren didn't lose any of those matches. So much for my influence!

I had to telephone Jimmy Bone right away to let him know the state of play. 'Are you sure, Chic?' he asked. I replied, 'I'm hardly likely to make something like this up, am I? I've got a broken leg.' Jimmy was fuming. 'Andy says it is just severe bruising.' 'Well, there's a guy wearing a white coat calling himself a doctor in a hospital who says it's a hairline fracture,' I answered. Jimmy's mood didn't get any better. 'I'm going to sack Andy,' he shouted. 'He's got to go. You've got a fuckin' broken leg and he can't diagnose that. He's no use to me. He's out of here.' I protested, 'It's not his fault, boss. Remember, I wasn't carried off the pitch – I did walk off, after all. Not too many guys with a broken leg do that.' I was fighting our physio's corner because I knew anyone could make a mistake. Jimmy calmed down. 'I'm going to reprimand him, then. He can't get away with it.' We both agreed a gentle boot up the backside might do the trick. Andy was a popular guy among the players at Love Street and, as I said, we used to wind him up something awful. He was one of those blokes whose face would go bright red in embarrassment if you pressed the right buttons. We were a rotten lot at Love Street. Maybe he got his revenge on me that afternoon at Stark's Park!

There was a guy called Tommy Cadberry who played for Rutherglen Glencairn when I was starting out. Tommy, who now runs that famous Celtic pub Bairds Bar in the Trongate in Glasgow, was afraid of nothing. He would have taken on Mike Tyson for a bet. I recall I was getting a hard time from a few fans during one game. They were heckling my every touch and, as a youngster, I have to admit it was a bit unsettling. Cad sidled over and said, 'I'm just going to have a word with your friends over there, OK?' He was heavily outnumbered, but that didn't faze Cad. He walked over to the touchline, made a couple of gestures and, lo and behold, there was nothing but silence from that section of the crowd for the remainder of the game. He never did tell me what he said, but it certainly had the desired effect!

I recall a story I heard about a Rangers player who was about to make his debut against Celtic at Ibrox a few years back. He was a foreigner and had heard all about the Glasgow derbies. He was desperate to get the fans on his side right from the off. 'How do I achieve this?' he asked a friend. 'Well, you could score a hat-trick, for a start,' he was told. 'Alternatively, you could clatter a Celtic player. That fans will love that.' The new boy took it on board and the game had hardly kicked off when the ball went to right-back Tommy Boyd, one of the nicest guys you'll meet in football. As Tommy brought the ball under control, he was hit by a whirlwind and ended up flat on his back on the track. The Rangers fans loved it and Gabriel Amato was an instant success in their eyes! The Argentine didn't score – it ended goalless, as I recall – but he had done the next best thing and flattened a Celtic player.

Davie Hay, my old boss at St Mirren, was known as The Quiet Assassin during his playing days and, as a kid, I saw quite a lot of him in action. No-one messed about with Davie. He was rock solid and I can remember some tasty Old Firm encounters when Jock Stein always put Davie into midfield. I was eleven years old when Davie left Celtic to go to Chelsea in 1974, but, even at a young age, I could appreciate his style of play. I played forty-two league games for him at the Paisley side and scored five goals. I know I could have done better, though.

John 'Cowboy' McCormack was coming to the end of his career when we were both at St Mirren. As a cheeky young lad I thought it would be a good idea to noise up the old pro in training. I was a bit lippy and I hit him a couple of times, but decided it would be a good idea to put the brakes on the challenges when he turned round and just gave me a stare that could have turned me to stone. He didn't need to boot me back – that glower did the trick. As I recall, there was also the little matter of being threatened with a belt round the ear. I didn't mess about with him after that.

John Lambie likes to tell everyone within earshot that he was a real hard man. He used to say to me, 'Chic, I would have cut you in two – you wouldn't have stood a chance. Lucky for you I wasn't around when you were playing.' My old Thistle gaffer used to insist, 'When I was out on that park even the worms were terrified to poke their heads above the surface.' He meant it, too! He often recalled playing for St Johnstone against the mighty Real Madrid at the Bernabeu in 1971. The Spanish giants were gearing up for the European Cup-Winners' Cup Final against Chelsea in Athens which was due the following week and apparently they wanted to play British opposition to get a feel for what they might expect.

John readily admits he kicked lumps out of their legendary left-winger Francisco Gento. I don't think the flying Spaniard is the forgiving kind because, according to John, Gento refused to shake hands or swap shirts at the end of the game which, by the way, the Saints lost 3-1. The Real Madrid icon was obviously the possessor of a good memory because he bumped into John years later at some sporting function and once again completely blanked him! 'He was still frightened of me,' boasted my old gaffer.

I don't think Jim Duffy ever got the praise he deserved for his skills and I'll tell you he could play a bit. That was surely emphasised when he won the Players' Player of the Year award at the end of season 1984/85 and, remember, he was playing for unfashionable Morton in the Premier League at the time. He could look after himself, too. He was so tough I don't recall him ever getting hurt in a challenge. There was one game when Partick Thistle were playing Clydebank at Kilbowie and if you've never been to this quaint little ground you will have to take my word for it that it is tight. Extremely tight and bordering on the downright dangerous with the walls surrounding the playing surface only a matter of yards from the touchline.

The Bankies used to have a player called Scott Murdoch and he thought he was a Jack-the-Lad and a bit tasty. Anyway, he and Duff were chasing a through pass and my mate was ahead of his opponent. Duff must have sensed what was coming next. Murdoch launched himself into a challenge that could have created problems for my pal. However, with immaculate timing, Duff swerved out of the way and the Clydebank player went sailing past him and thudded straight into the wall. He should have known better. That was the end of the game for him as the stretcher bearers were called on.

Two other Partick Thistle players who could handle themselves were Steve Pittman and Alan Dinnie. Pitts already had a bit of a reputation when he joined us from Dundee and he, too, could combine talent with tenacity. He didn't take too many prisoners, as I recall. Pitts was a particular friend of mine and I crashed out at his house in Pumpherston on more than a few occasions. Pitts, his wife Izzy and I would do our best to lower the European vodka lake and, inevitably, I would conk out on their couch in the front room. Mind you, I didn't get too much sleep because of those bloody aeroplanes flying in and out of Edinburgh. Dinnie was exactly the same as Pitts. They could dish it out, but they could also take it and I can tell you there were never any grudges after a game. Back then, though, you couldn't blame our opponents for wondering what lay in store for them at Firhill when they were about to face a bunch of renegades!

As a Celtic fan, I thoroughly enjoyed watching Murdo MacLeod in action. He is a good friend today, but that is not clouding my judgement. He was known as The Rhino the way he charged around the pitch. He was a powerful figure of a man, but he had a terrific touch, too. I remember the time George Best was playing for Hibs in a Scottish Cup semi-final against Celtic at Hampden in 1980. George, of course, was coming to the end of an illustrious career and had been lured north by the Easter Road chairman Tom Hart, picking up something like £5,000-per-week. That would have been a small fortune away back then. Anyway, George picked up a loose ball, steadied himself, looked around to see what pass was on and the next thing he knew he was crashing to the turf. He had just met The Rhino. Murdo, no respecter of reputations obviously, came in like a whirlwind, flatted the Northern Ireland icon and took off with the ball in the opposite direction.

Murdo was cute, too. He knew when to leave his foot in a tackle just to put down a marker. Never dirty, but a great man to have in your team. I've got to know Murdo really well with the work we do for Maximise, a company run by Coca-Cola to help youngsters hone their skills at parks up and down the country. Normally before the kids turn up to go through a session Murdo and I will have a wee kickabout between ourselves as we limber up. Just to put an edge of proceedings I said to him once, 'I can do anything you can do.' Murdo smiled and asked, 'Can you pick up league titles? Can you pick up Scottish Cups? Can you pick up League Cups? Can you score the winner in a Cup Final? Can you play for Scotland in the World Cup Finals?' Of course, Murdo had achieved all that and more. I had no answer to any of that. I don't think he was overly impressed when I pointed out that I had, in fact, won the Glasgow Cup with Partick Thistle!

11

ME AND MY MADCAP MATES

I believe it wouldn't be a massive understatement or a gross exaggeration to say I have come across some madcap pals on my travels through football. For a start, there's a bloke called Brian Gallagher, a former team-mate at Partick Thistle, who really shouldn't be allowed to eat with sharp implements. In fact, this bloke should carry a Government Health Warning stamped across his forehead. Gal, as he is known to everyone, is actually quite a bright bloke and was educated at St Mungo's Academy in Glasgow where you require more than one lonely little grey cell to mix in that company. So, he does possess a brain and is fairly smart although I have to say his disguise is perfect!

I'll give you an example. Big Gal was regularly in and out of hospitals with a variety of skin complaints. Once they kept him in for a few nights at Stobhill, but, as you will discover, even these sedate surroundings couldn't keep my pal out of mischief. I visited him on a few occasions and there was no point in bringing in grapes or fruit for Gal – it had to be a six-pack of beer and a couple of bottles of cider. We used to smuggle them in and Gal would make a beeline for the TV room to make short work of our 'gifts'.

There was an old bloke in a bed opposite Gal in the ward and one night my pal thought it would be a good idea to play a trick on him. The old fellow must have taken a sedative or something because he was quite drowsy on this particular evening. Gal, obviously bored, got up in the middle of the night and found a doctor's coat from somewhere. He tiptoed over to his fellow-patient's bed and nudged him. The old chap was in a deep sleep and slowly came round and opened his eyes to be confronted with what he thought was a doctor. We'll call the old chap Mr Smith. Gal shook him and said,'Mr Smith, waken up. This is Doctor Gallagher and I am afraid I have got some very bad news for you.' The old guy, still half-asleep, asked, 'Yes, doctor, what is it?' Gal kept a straight and solemn face. 'I'm sorry, Mr Smith, but I will have to take off your leg tomorrow. I will have to amputate just above the right knee. I will perform the operation in the morning. Don't worry and get a good night's sleep.'

The guy must have been on something fairly strong because he did fall asleep again. Gal sneaked back to his bed to await the reaction of his ward mate in the morning. The doctors were doing their early rounds when the old chap awakened. Suddenly the full horror of the news that he had been told by 'Doctor Gallagher' sunk in. He started screaming at the docs and nurses, 'You can't take off my leg. I'm only in here with a skin infection. There's nothing wrong with my leg. You can't take it off. Leave me alone!' The medical staff were more than just a little bemused, as you might imagine. Gal had his head under the sheets by this time as the docs said, 'What on earth are you havering about? Why on earth would we take off your leg? We're letting you out tomorrow.'

The old fella wasn't convinced and Gal told me he was still blethering on about the docs cutting off his leg by the time his family came visiting. 'They want to take off my leg,' he told them. 'I've only got a skin complaint and they want to take off my leg.' His son looked at him and said, 'Dad, have you been at the drink again?'

Then there was the night when I was settling down to watch

the European Championship Final between France and Italy in 2000. I had my feet up and was about to get a cold bottle of beer from the fridge when the telephone shrilled. 'Who the hell's that?' I thought, but answered it just the same. It was Gal and he was in Stobhill again. 'Chic, I need cider,' he said fairly frantically. 'Can you get me some cider? Now!' I pleaded with my mate, 'C'mon, Gal, I'm just about to watch the European Championship Final.' It didn't dissuade Gal from the notion that I had to get to the off-licence, pick up a couple of bottles of cider and hotfoot it over to the hospital to deliver the goods.

I had a brainwave. 'Gal, I've no money,' I said. 'I'm sorry, but it will have to wait until tomorrow.' Gal was having none of it. 'I'll pay you when you get here. I need cider. Now!' Reluctantly, I switched off the TV, got into my car, picked up the cider and took the bottles over to Stobhill. An auxiliary nurse came down and collected them. She then handed me about four quid in two pence pieces! Cheers, Gal.

When I was starting out at Rutherglen Glencairn I was very friendly with one of the players called Eddie Lepkowski. Actually, I was best man at his wedding. Like Gal, Eddie was blessed – or cursed, if you prefer – with a weird sense of humour. The boss at the Glens was a guy called John Houston and his assistant was ex-Celtic player Willie O'Neill. Anyway, John was as enthusiastic as they came. He was quite thorough and meticulous in his team talks. Honestly, it could have been Sir Alex Ferguson getting Manchester United prepared for a Champions League Final. He took everything so seriously.

One day he was going through his usual tactic talks and at the end asked, 'Anyone got any questions?' Normally, no-one had any queries. We just wanted to get out there and get stuck into the action. John surveyed the players in front of him and his eyes lit up when Eddie said, 'Aye, boss, I've got a question.' At last, someone was going to put John's tactical knowledge to

the test. Enthusiastically, he said, 'OK, Eddie, what is it?' He was eager in anticipation. 'Where did you get that fuckin' duffel coat?' asked Eddie.

Davie Hay wasn't too pleased with me and a few of my team-mates when he took St Mirren to Spain for a break before we were due to play Dundee United at Tannadice. Davie, one of the nicest guys you will ever meet, trained us on the Monday, but gave the players the following day off. He warned us, 'Make sure you are back at the hotel for midnight. No-one stays out after twelve o'clock. Understood?' We nodded in agreement. Kenny McDowall, now a first team coach at Rangers, Roddy Manley, Alan Irvine, Julian Broddle and yours truly duly set up camp at a bar not far from the hotel.

Across the road at another bar were assistant manager Gordon Smith, now chief executive at the SFA, and Roy Aitken, who was player/coach with the Saints. As the midnight hour approached, Gordon came over to our bar to tell us to remember the curfew. Fairly unreasonably, upon reflection, we pointed out that Big Roy was still a player and he, too, should observe Davie Hay's orders. It didn't matter to us that he was on the management side. After a few bevvies this made sense to all of us. Gordon shrugged his shoulders and said, 'OK, lads, you've been told. It's up to you.' To a man, we decided it was a wonderful idea to keep on drinking.

I was rooming with Kenny McDowall at the time and the following morning I awoke and said, 'I think we got away with it, Kenny.' He looked at me and replied, 'What are you talking about? Davie Hay was sitting in the foyer when we eventually got back to the hotel. Don't you remember going over to him and knocking off his baseball cap? You asked him if he wasn't happy with us. I think you can safely say he was far from delighted with the lot of us.'

Sure enough, the St Mirren gaffer called the five of us over

before breakfast and informed us we were going to be fined two weeks' wages – about £800 in my case. The players were just a bit taken aback. One of us said, 'Boss, don't you think that's just a wee bit over the top?' Davie thought for a moment and came back with, 'If you beat Dundee United on Saturday I'll only dock you your win bonus money. Does that sound fair?' We agreed. However, he added, 'Lose and I'll fine you a fortnight's wages.' The bonus was £400 and we realised we could live without that just so long as there was no pay deduction. Needless to say, we were a team possessed against a very good Dundee United side on their own ground. We hammered them 4-1 and I came on as a substitute and scored a goal. I'll tell you this – we would have beaten Real Madrid and Barcelona that day!

There was another amusing incident with Davie Hay, who paid almost £300,000 to sign me and my pal David Elliot from Partick Thistle. I was suspended and would have to sit out the Saturday game. Davie, quite rightly, thought I should attend, anyway, and show face. I conjured up some sort of excuse that got me out of attending. There was an Old Firm game on that weekend and that's where yours truly was heading to give my vocal support to Celtic.

I came in for training on Monday and Davie asked me to have a word with him in his office. Surely I hadn't been rumbled? Davie looked stern as I popped my head around the door and said, 'You want to see me, boss?' 'Come in,' ordered Davie. I walked in, took a seat and the gaffer asked, 'Where were you on Saturday?' I lied, 'Sorry I missed the game, boss, but I had some important business to take care of at home. It took me all day.' Davie fixed me in his gaze and slowly reached for a news-paper. He opened it at the appropriate page in the sports section, turned it round for me to look at, pointed to a photograph and said, 'That guy in the crowd at the Old Firm game looks helluva like you, don't you think?' I looked at the photo. I was done like

a kipper. There I was sitting in the stand with the rest of the Celtic supporters. I don't think my boss was greatly impressed. Bloody photographers!

Davie was a marvellous guy to work for and with, but I recall a game where he actually ordered me back into the dug-out after telling me to go out and limber up in preparation for going on as a substitute. It was a rain-lashed day in Paisley and Rangers just happened to be our opponents. We were playing quite well and were holding our own. It was goalless and the Rangers support were strangely muted. Until I made my appearance. Davie told me to warm up and, as you might expect, I headed straight to where most of the travelling support was that day. I was winding them up big-style and suddenly they found their voices. I gave them a new lease of life, unfortunately. Davie leapt out of the dug-out and frantically waved at me to return. Too late. The Rangers fans were in full swing now and their vociferous backing backfired on us. They ended up winning 3-0 and Davie turned to me and said, 'It's all your fault. They were half-asleep until you appeared.' I couldn't argue.

First time around at Love Street, I used to travel through to Paisley with Frank McAvennie and Frank McDougall, who smoked about five cigarettes each during a relatively short journey. I enjoyed their company and we still keep in touch. Frank McDougall now owns a bar in Aberdeen and I've been up to see him on a few occasions. I was involved in the John Lambie Testimonial Committee a few years back when I contacted Sir Alex Ferguson's PA at Old Trafford to see if we could get a signed Manchester United shirt to put up for auction at John's function. To be fair, Sir Alex telephoned me right back and agreed to send up a top autographed by Wayne Rooney and he was as good as his word. While I was talking to the United boss he enquired, 'Do you still keep in touch with Frank McDougall?' Frank, of course, had played for Sir Alex at Aberdeen and I recall

him scoring four goals against Celtic and then three against Rangers in back-to-back games. 'Yes,' I answered, 'we're still friends.'

Sir Alex then recalled taking a phone call from Frank who was living in Bury at the time and running a Sunday morning pub team. Frank was looking for advice from his mentor. 'I've got this really good player,' he said. 'He's the best in the team, but I've got a problem with him. He turns up one week and doesn't the next. I've had words with him, but he is just ignoring me. What can I do?' Sir Alex thought for a moment and asked, 'What age is he?' Frank answered, 'He's thirty-nine.' Fergie fired back, 'Tell him to get to fuck!'

I was a regular passenger in Barry Lavety's car when we were at Hibs. David Elliot was another who got a lift to training. Barry would always go on about this wonderful girlfriend of his. She was perfect in his eyes. One day I asked him for his mobile phone. I said, 'I'll telephone your girlfriend, Barry, and tell her how much she means to you.' Barry thought it was a great idea. He handed me the phone, I hit the speed dial and, sure enough, on came the love of Barry's life. I said, 'Hello, you don't know me, but I've noticed you working in a hairdressers. I got your number from a friend and I hope you don't mind me calling you. I wouldn't normally do this, but I wondered if you were seeing anyone special at the moment.'

Back came the reply, 'No, there's nothing serious just now.' I cracked up. She had been going out with Barry for about four years and he was mesmerised by her. Obviously, my team-mate didn't hear the conversation and I hung up and handed him back his phone. Barry asked, 'What did she say, Chic?' I couldn't possibly tell him the truth. I lied, 'She says you are special to her, too, Barry.' He smiled and said, 'I told you she was a good girl.' If only he knew.

We had a bloke at St Mirren who indulged in a recreational

drug or two. I can't name him for legal reasons or the fact he might turn up at my front door with a baseball bat! He was a youngster who enjoyed the disco life. He went to all those rave things and when the referee used to blow the whistle to start the game I swear he started to dance!

There was another day when Gerry Collins was driving me and a bloke called Stevie Evans back from training at Ayr United. It was a dreadful evening and we got caught in a blizzard on Fenwick Moor. Trust me, there are better places to break down in the snow, but that's exactly what happened to us. Nightmare! Gerry said, 'Don't panic, I've got a pal who'll come to the rescue.' He used his mobile to make his plea and said with a satisfied grin, 'He's on his way. He'll be here in about half an hour.' I said, 'He must be a special pal if he's willing to come out in this.' Gerry smiled, 'Oh, he's special alright.' True to his word, his mate turned up about twenty minutes or so later. I was stunned to see it was none other than Tommy Burns, the Celtic legend. I was about twenty years old at the time, totally in awe of the guy and could hardly believe it when he gave us all a lift home. It was an overwhelming gesture by one of life's true gentlemen. Mind you, we still had a tussle or two together later on during our playing days!

Frank McAvennie, as I said, is still a good pal, but if you want to drive John Lambie crazy just mention his name. The boss thought he had pulled off a signing coup when he got in touch with my old mate and had talks about joining Thistle. Macca turned up, verbally agreed on a deal and was photographed at Firhill wearing a Thistle top and holding up a club scarf. Lambie was delighted. However, while Macca was being paraded – much the same way as Mo Johnston was at Celtic before he infamously defected to Rangers in 1989 – he received a telephone call from his agent Bill McMurdo, who, ironically, was involved in Mo's move to Ibrox.

'Celtic want to sign you,' he was told by McMurdo. Liam Brady, then the Parkhead manager, was short of strikers and he thought a second stint in the Hoops for Macca would be a good move. What was my pal to do? Partick Thistle or Celtic? Unfortunately, for John Lambie, he hadn't actually signed any forms. He was still free to do what he wanted. Of course, he rejoined Celtic. Macca, to this day, still asks me, 'Has John Lambie forgiven me yet?' I tell him, 'If you value your health it's probably wise you give John a wide berth. He still wants to belt you!'

By the way, John Lambie, as you will surely have gathered, is still a special friend to me. However, I have to correct him on one point. He often tells people, 'See that Chic Charnley, do you know he can't sleep at night? Why? Well, he knows there are pubs still open in Australia.' Not true!

Macca and I have shifted an ale or two in our time. I like his company and he is a marvellous storyteller. Of course, when he was at Celtic he used to drive Billy McNeill up the wall. He was always late for training on a Monday because he had missed his flight up from London. He was going out with Page Three model Jenny Blyth at the time and would head for England's capital as soon as the final whistle went on the game on a Saturday. So, Billy kept fining him for his timekeeping. Macca had to find away around this, but he wasn't about to give up his weekends in Stringfellows. On the other hand, he couldn't afford to keep on shelling out for fines.

What to do? Macca hit upon a bright idea – well, there's always a first time! – and got in touch with a bloke called Captain George who worked for a radio station. He was in the helicopter that flew over Glasgow to give out up-to-date road reports, where there was congestion and so on. It was known as the Eye in the Sky. He had a spot at Glasgow Airport before going out on his rounds and he would return there every now and again. Macca spotted the helicopter one day as he tried to get to training for 10am. In typical fashion, my good mate approached Captain George. 'How about we strike up a wee deal?' he said to the intrigued radio man. 'Can you get me to Barrowfield in this thing in about ten minutes?' Captain George was one who liked a challenge. 'Let's give it a whirl,' he replied. They took off, Macca got in touch with team-mate Derek Whyte to look out his gear and he would meet him at the training ground. Sure enough, the helicopter made it to Barrowfield on time and Macca was saved another hit in the pocket. He's not as daft as he looks that boy! Mind you, he was in such a rush to scramble out the copter before Billy McNeill arrived that he almost tripped and broke his neck. I am assured that Captain George rescued Macca on more than one occasion with this excellent ploy. It's always good to have pals in high places!

There was another occasion when Dundee's Barry Smith thought I was going off my head. Barry used to pick me up and take me to training at Dens Park. I phoned him one morning to say I couldn't make it and not to waste his time coming for me. There was a moment's silence and Barry came back with, 'Chic, you left Dundee three months ago for Hibs. Don't you remember?' Yes, I had telephoned the wrong Barry. By this time, of course, it was Barry Lavety who was very kindly giving me lifts to Easter Road in the morning. I had to work hard to persuade Barry Smith I wasn't going doolally.

It hasn't always been fun and games and I recall an evening when I was with Dundee and my colleagues were threatening to string up one of their team-mates. Dariusz Adamczuk, who would later join Rangers, was playing cards with a few of the Dundee boys while they were on a tour of Ireland. He had a few quid after playing for Italian side Udinese in the Serie A and he was adding to his pile by winning just about every game of cards. I wasn't playing, but Paul Tosh came to me and said, 'Chic, do us a favour, will you? We think Adamczuk is cheating. Will you keep an eye on him for us?'

Players can lose their wages in games like these when things get out of hand. I agreed to have a look on their behalf. I gave the lads the nod and one of them lifted the Pole right out of his seat. Cards were found under his seat and the players just about went berserk. If they had had a rope in their possession at that moment Adamczuk would have been found dangling from a lamppost the following day! They were all for giving him a right good hiding. Adamczuk realised he had been rumbled and admitted his folly. John McCormack ordered a team meeting before any punishment was meted out.

Eventually, the Dundee players calmed down, but only if Adamczuk paid back his winnings. Guys were coming forward and claiming they had lost all sorts of money and, in the end, Adamczuk ended up shelling out more dosh than he actually won. He wasn't complaining, though. At least his head was still attached to his neck.

Although I have had a few run-ins with John McVeigh I would still rate him as a pal. He was involved in that football movie *A Shot At Glory* which was made by American actor Robert Duvall, famous for his roles in *The Godfather* movies. Duvall, for this film, collected a pile of footballers to play for a wee team that gets to the Scottish Cup Final. Rangers' Ally McCoist got the main role and, knowing him, he probably demanded star billing! Duvall and Co were using Firhill when they were filming training and the Hollywood legend ended up in the heart of Possil one morning when they couldn't gain access to Thistle's ground.

A lovely lady called Brenda was the Firhill keyholder and she hadn't turned up one day. It appeared no-one else had a key. John McVeigh had the solution. 'I know where Brenda stays in Possil. I'll drive over there just now and pick up the keys.' Duvall, rather surprisingly, agreed to join John in the drive through Glasgow. They duly arrived at the close where Brenda stayed and Duvall must have thought he was back in the Bronx. There was graffiti everywhere as he and John made their way to Brenda's door. They rang the bell. No answer. They rattled on the door. Still no answer.

Suddenly there was a voice coming from the stairwell above them. A young boy was peering down and asked, 'Are you looking for Brenda?' 'Aye,' said John. 'You've just missed her, mister. She left about five minutes ago.' The lad must have been a fan of films because he actually recognised Duvall. 'Hey, are you that wee fuckin' actor?' he queried. Duvall agreed he was indeed that 'wee fuckin' actor'. John and the movie icon were walking out the close when they heard the plea from behind them, 'Gonnae lend me a tenner, pal?'

Talking of Ally McCoist, he once got me a beauty when I was involved with that company called Maximise, run by a great lad called Charlie Mularvey, and I was taking some kids for training at Hampden. It's something I really enjoy and I've spent some good times with youngsters working for the Coca-Cola Sevens. Walter Kidd and Gary Mackay used to be sworn enemies out on the football field during our playing days when they were with Hearts and I was in opposition. There was never any quarter asked or given. However, they are also involved with Maximise and we've been together as we've trained the kids. They are now friends. On this particular day, we were giving the lads a work-out when Ally turned up at the national stadium. I could hear this shout coming down from the top of one of the stands, 'Hey, Charnley, I see you've got to play at Hampden at last.' I'll get him back for that; watch this space!

The comedian Andy Cameron is another True Blue and I've bumped into him on a few charity occasions. Andy may be a Rangers fan, but he is not blinkered. He has appeared at loads of Celtic functions and was there on 24 May 2009 for a night to honour Stevie Chalmers, the player, of course, who scored the most important goal in the club's history; the winner in the 2-1 European Cup Final victory over Inter Milan in Lisbon in 1967. What was special that evening at Celtic Park was the fact that Rangers had won the league that afternoon for the first time in four years when they beat Dundee United 3-0 at Tannadice and Celtic drew 0-0 with Hearts in Glasgow. Could anyone have blamed Andy for wanting to be elsewhere that night? However, he had promised to turn up for Stevie's big night and, to his eternal credit, he refused to go back on his word. I remember I was at a function with Andy when I had to autograph something. Andy held it up, looked at it and declared, 'My God, Chic even signs his name in Latin!'

Andy, of course, does a lot of charity work, irrespective of religion. He's a good bluenose – can there be such a thing? – but he is no bigot. I recall a story after he had agreed to host a night for a Catholic church fundraiser. A week before the show, the church had been broken into and some articles had been stolen. Anyway, Andy walked into the church and looked up at a statue of Christ on the cross. 'I see you got the guy who robbed you,' he said. You'll pay for that on Judgement Day, Andy!

There is one bloke who is still a pal, but I wouldn't have blamed him one bit if he had never spoken to me again in his life. Well, I did contrive to ruin his football career, didn't I? His name was John Hynd – or Hyndo, as everyone calls him – and I was a team-mate of his at Possil Villa. We were told a scout from Rutherglen Glencairn was coming to take in a game this particular weekend. You won't be surprised to learn that I was suspended. I was desperate to play, though, and, amazingly, the bosses agreed. I had to take Hyndo's identity, though, and he was dropped. Thankfully, he agreed and Chic Charnley was transformed into John Hynd for the match.

It was all going swimmingly until the red mist came down.

The referee was annoying the hell out of me and eventually I snapped. I went for him and had to be dragged away by my team-mates. The authorities at that level were not too happy and slapped a one year's suspension on poor Hyndo! That was bad enough, but he also worked in a brewery and, with no activity at the weekend or training during the week for a full twelve months, he sampled his company's wares to extent that, at the age of twenty-four, he ballooned to about eighteen stone! By the time the ban was up, he was completely unfit and couldn't run the length of himself. His wife Anne Marie never did see the funny side of the entire incident and I can't say I blame her.

Bertie Auld is a legend and was a special talent when I was watching Celtic as a kid. Being a left-footer, I watched in awe as Bertie slung passes all over the place with impeccable accuracy. Wee Jinky was my main man, but Bertie was right up there, too. I'm delighted to say Bertie is still a friend to this day and we have had some interesting experiences together. I was a guest at Celtic Park for a Champions League game against Benfica in 2007. I was in a sponsors' box when Bertie barged in and saw me. 'Oh, God, they're letting anyone in now,' he exclaimed. He came in, grabbed me by the arm and said, 'There's someone you have got to meet.'

He dragged me off to another box and there was the legendary Eusebio. I was barely out of my nappies when the magnificent Portuguese superstar – and I use the word in its proper sense – was terrorising defences in the sixties. This may surprise you, but I spend a lot of time studying football footage from all sorts of eras and Eusebio was the player of the tournament during the 1966 World Cup Finals in England. He was simply playing football from another planet. Watch him against North Korea in the quarter-finals and you'll see what I mean. The Koreans raced into a three goal lead and one of those freak results that crop up every now and again looked on the cards. Enter Eusebio. He rattled in four goals and Jose Torres added another as Portugal romped to an emphatic 5-3 triumph.

The man was a truly gifted footballer and here I was being presented to him by Bertie Auld. 'Hey, Eusebio,' said Bertie with that impish grin of his. 'This is a pal of mine called Chic Charnley.' Eusebio, slightly bemused, shook my hand and, naturally enough, had never heard of me. I doubt very much if he even knew what a Partick Thistle was! As this genuine legend greeted me, Bertie added, 'Do you know something Eusebio? Chic was a better player than you!' Praise indeed. Not true, of course, but I basked in the sentiment for all of five seconds.

I thrive in Bertie's company. We had a wonderful time in Benidorm a few years ago when we tried to drink the place dry. I've got a pal called Ger Mulcahey who runs a fabulous boozer called The Friar's Walk Tavern in Cork. I get on really well with Ger's brother Paul, but he is another dangerous guy to know. I have never got out of Cork sober after nights out with this guy. Anyway, a friend of Ger, Jim Twigg, was running a Celtic convention in the Spanish holiday resort and we were put together by Ger. He wanted to run it along the lines of the hugely successful Las Vegas Celtic Convention that brings in fans from all over the globe. Anyway, he telephoned me to see if I would be interested in putting together an ex-Celtic team to play in Benidorm. Originally, it was to be five-a-sides, but, as things progressed, we got to a full complement of eleven and we were to play a Benidorm Select.

I knew Jim was being well weighed in by the local authorities and he offered me £1,000 for each of the players I took over. It sounded ideal. A holiday in the sun and all we had to do was kick a ball about for ninety minutes and meet and greet the fans. I would have done it for nothing. I got in touch with Bertie to see if he would be interested in becoming the team manager. 'No problem,' said Bertie. Then I got in touch with the likes of Frank McAvennie, Mark McNally, Willie McStay and George and

Pat McCluskey among others. Dixie Deans came along in some capacity, Brian Gallagher was kitman and another friend, Steven Milne, travelled, too. By the way, Steven and I were in business together a few years ago after taking over the Thistle Bar close to Firhill. That was too much like hard work. I know which side of the bar I prefer to be on.

Jim Twigg counted out sixteen envelopes and each was supposed to contain £1,000 or the equivalent in Euros. He handed me a plastic bag and said, 'I'll leave it to you, Chic, to distribute the cash among your pals.' That evening Macca and the others came to the room I was sharing with Gal. I duly dished out the cash. However, I could only find fifteen envelopes, one was missing. I would take it up with Jim later. A few minutes later one of the boys came back to me to say their envelope was a couple of hundred Euros short. Then another arrived with the same complaint. To be fair to Jim, he addressed the problem immediately and made up the agreed totals. However, I was still an envelope short and £1,000 down on the deal. Jim might have been puzzled, but he put together another envelope with the correct amount of cash and everyone was happy.

I was in the room shortly afterwards when Gal's mobile phone started ringing. I was turning the place upside down trying to find the phone when I came across the missing envelope. It must have fallen out of the plastic bag and got lodged underneath a bed. I checked the contents and, sure enough, there was £1,000 worth of Euros. My immediate thought – honest! – was to give it back to Jim Twigg. At that point Gal entered the room and I said, 'Gal, I've found the missing cash. There were sixteen envelopes, after all. I'll hand it back to Jim.' Gal was having none of that. 'He's getting a fortune for hosting this event,' said my mate. 'Don't be daft. Let's go for a drink.' I contacted Bertie, Gal and Mark McNally. Along with a girl called Marion, sister of Ger Mulcahey, we found a convenient bar.

I put £300 through the door of Steven Milne to give him some spending money and I took the £700 balance to the bar. I think we stayed there for two days! We were all doing our best to get through this extra cash and the champagne was flowing. At one point Marion looked at her watch and said, 'It's ten o'clock. Is this morning or night-time?' Honestly, she didn't have a clue. We had to think hard before we gave her an answer! Mark was so dehydrated we had to take him to hospital.

We had a fantastic time and I thoroughly enjoyed playing against the Benidorm Select. As there is no footage of the game you will have to take my word for it that I scored a goal from inside my own half. I received a pass, spotted the goalkeeper had strayed to the edge of his penalty box and I flighted an effort towards his goal. He looked horrified when he realised he was in imminent danger of conceding a goal and he did his best to scramble back to clear the effort. Too late. The ball sailed serenely over his head and was nestling in the net before he could get into position. I think that deserved £1,000 on its own!

Sadly, the Benidorm convention didn't quite take off in the same manner as the Las Vegas equivalent. Unfortunately, a lot of the stalls selling all sorts of Celtic stuff were about ten miles out of the city centre and the fans preferred to stay in the vicinity and enjoy a refreshment or two.

I must make an apology to Joe McBride here and now. Joe, one of the greatest goalscorers in Celtic history, went as a guest of the sponsors. He should have been with us and it was my fault he had been overlooked when I was putting the squad together. Oops! I would much have preferred to give him £1,000 to be our kitman. He would have done a better job than Gal. Mind you, that wouldn't have been too difficult!

Speaking of Vegas reminds of one of the times I was over there with my Celtic mates. We were walking past this bar when I heard a shout, 'One-game wonder!' I looked around and there was Bertie beaming back. 'One-game wonder,' he repeated with obvious reference to my appearance against Manchester United. He added, 'And you were lucky to get that one game.' I tried to stay out of his way for the rest of the jaunt.

There was a bit of a drinking club at Firhill – shock! horror! – and we used some of the local hostelries after training. I can recall on more than a few occasions about eleven or twelve of us setting off for a quick one before going home. Most of us were lucky if we got out of the pub before midnight! My mates Alan Dinnie and Steve Pittman liked a refreshment. There was one famous day when they walked into the Saracen Bar in Possil and startled the barman by ordering twenty vodkas. Then they went for a drink!

I enjoyed a drink, too, of course, and a night out with the lads. I recall an evening when we all rolled up at the Savoy Nightclub in Glasgow's Sauchiehall Street. Imagine my surprise when I bumped into my Ma who was out with some friends on a hen night. At the end of the evening, I arranged to get a taxi for my Ma and me to make sure we both got home safely. As we were walking down the stairs I heard one of my mates say, 'Look at Chic – he's pulled an old bird!'

Being the nice lad that I am, I once spotted a mate of mine, Billy Kelly, standing at a bus stop in Barmulloch along with his sister. I was driving past and pulled over. 'Hop in,' I said, 'I'll give you a lift.' I thought they might be going somewhere local in Springburn. 'Where are you heading?' Billy didn't hesitate, 'East Kilbride'. East bloody Kilbride! I had put £40 on a horse running in the Derby that day and was hoping to get settled in front of the telly to see how it performed. Unless my car could be transformed into a James Bond-type jet plane that wasn't going to happen. Eventually, I drove them to their destination, went to a bookies and discovered that my luck hadn't changed and my horse had lost. So, that was forty quid down the drain and I was out about £20 in petrol. You get days like that, don't you?

Talking of gambling, here's a wee story I was told by Billy about his brother John Kelly who was on Celtic's books back in the Fifties. Apparently, he was known as Non-Stop Kelly, but he didn't really make the grade at Parkhead. He went down to England for a trial with some club and, to pass some time on Friday night, he went to the greyhounds. It was an innocent way of whiling away the hours before his outing on the Saturday. He got talking to this chap who gave him a tip for a dog. 'Can't lose,' said Non-Stop's new mate. Sure enough, it won. Non-Stop was so pleased that he took the bloke to the bar for a whisky. They came out for the next race and once again a tip was forthcoming and, believe it or not, it won again. It was back to the bar for Non-Stop and his chum for another round of whiskies. This went on all the way through the card and it would be fair to say that Non-Stop might not have been too steady on his feet at the end of the evening. He went to his hotel to sleep it off and get prepared for his trial the following day. Non-Stop duly turned up at the ground and was milling around when he spotted his good friend from the night before. He walked over and said, 'What are you doing here?' The smile on the face of his tipster turned to a scowl. He said, 'I'm the chairman and we don't need your likes at this club.' With that, Non-Stop was on his way back up the road, the trial scrapped.

I recall an evening when I was on the after dinner circuit. I was at the top table with a variety of guests, including the former Liverpool player Ronnie Whelan. Before the start of the speeches, the announcer stood up to introduce us. He said, 'Tonight we have a special guest in Ronnie Whelan. He's won trophies all over the place. He's got European Cup medals, English league title medals, League Cup medals and FA Cup medals. He's played for the Republic of Ireland and he's been one of the best players in Liverpool's history. He's got more medals than Montgomery.' There was a round of applause from the audience. The announcer continued, 'And we've also got Chic Charnley.' Swiftly he added, 'He's won fuck all!' Thanks, mate.

I've remained in touch with the guys I grew up with in Possil and one good friend was a bloke called Peter Gibson. He had a young son by the same name and he became a Partick Thistle supporter. He used to hang around outside Firhill on matchday with his friends. I used to collect tickets for the games and give them away. One day young Peter was there and he shouted over, 'Tell my mates that you are my uncle.' Obviously, he had been bragging about his Uncle Chic who played for the mighty Partick Thistle. I walked over and said, 'Yes, that's right and Peter is my favourite nephew.' You could see the relief on the kid's face because he had come so close to be caught out in a lie. And with that I made his day by handing him four spare tickets.

I had several interesting relatives I really liked as I was growing up and there was Uncle William who was more like a big brother to me. God only knows how many fights I got him into! Luckily enough, my uncle, who was only about six years older than me, was fairly handy when it came to fisticuffs, so his good looks were preserved.

Alan Dinnie, my old chum at Thistle, is still a genuine pal and he hasn't had his problems to seek after quitting football. Alan even ended up getting a custodial sentence at that grey, old fortress called Barlinnie Prison in Glasgow after getting caught with drugs. It says a lot for John Lambie and Jim Duffy, two Premier League managers at the time, that they visited him on a regular basis. I went, too, and I really felt for my pal. John, Jim and myself might not have agreed with Alan's actions, but we weren't going to turn our backs on him when he needed us most. I'm glad to say he has now sorted himself out.

I couldn't possibly close this chapter without going into depth on Jim Duffy. He is still a great friend and we play tennis every now and again. Although I have to say it is getting boring now as I rack up victory after victory. I have got Duff to thank for extending my playing career by about two years, at least. I was merely going through the motions at Dumbarton in 1995 and, if I'm being honest, I had lost my edge. It was difficult to work up any great enthusiasm for playing for The Sons and I mean absolutely no disrespect to anyone at the club by admitting that. It just happens to be the truth. That's why I didn't hesitate when Duff got in touch to enquire if I would be interested in joining Dundee. Interested? Try and stop me.

I think Duff paid £25,000 for me, so all parties concerned were satisfied. Duff, of course, had been a team-mate at Partick Thistle, so he knew fine well what to expect from me. He was brought up in Maryhill, not far from myself. I held no surprises for him. Some of the Dundee players asked another former Firhill colleague, Gerry Britton, about me. Obviously, my reputation went before me. Gerry, thankfully, told my soon-to-be new mates that I was OK. Imagine their surprise, then, when I turned up for my first day at training with a lovely black eye. I had got into a slight altercation with a resident from Possil the night before and was punched flush in the eye. There was no disguising the bruising, either. I don't think they were going to swallow the 'I walked into a door' routine.

I don't believe they were too impressed, either, when I got lost trying to get to Dundee to make my debut. I took every wrong turning that was possible, but, as kick-off for a game against Hamilton Accies got closer, I became more and more frantic. Thankfully, I made it on time and Duff accepted my reason. He played me from the start and I scored the winning goal in a 2-1 triumph. It was an absolute screamer, too, as I recall. It was a goal the minute it left my boot and Accies boss Iain Munro was kind enough to say afterwards that his team had lost to a wonder strike.

Duff was as hard as nails. We got on well enough, but he didn't accept any crap from anyone. We were in Ireland for a pre-season tour when I witnessed my old mate in full flow. I can't remember who we were playing, but it would be fair to say we weren't exactly putting our backs into it. It was merely an exercise to get our fitness levels up and, obviously, the result didn't matter. Or so we thought. We went in goalless at half-time.

Our boss was in a rage. He stormed into the dressing room and gave us all pelters. He went through us all individually and was finding it difficult to control his anger. I don't think I had ever seen him like that before. He then turned on me and I wasn't going to be spared, friend or not. He had his rant and I hit back, 'Fuck off, Duff.' He just about blew a fuse. 'No, you fuck off,' he fired back. 'In fact, get your kit off, you're not playing in the second-half.' I was standing right beside the door leading to the tunnel and didn't make a move. A few moments later the referee gave us the nod to go out for the second-half. Before Duff could say or do anything, I was down the tunnel and onto the pitch for the second forty-five minutes. He must have calmed down because he left me on. Believe me, everyone put in a fair bit of effort in that period and we won by a few.

I apologised to the boss afterwards and he accepted it. 'Just don't let it happen again, Chic. Okay?' I agreed it wasn't the done thing to swear at the gaffer. That was the spat finished there and then. Duff was never one to hold grudges. It was over and done with and there wouldn't be any silly reprisals. Duff is a man's man and I would trust him with my life. I really mean that.

Duff still has the rare distinction of sending me off during training! He spotted I was getting involved with a Dundee colleague and he knew what would inevitably follow. Before we came to blows, he called me over and said, 'I'm ordering you off, Chic. Go and have a bath and calm down.' I didn't need to protest. He had made up his mind and he wasn't going to change it. I walked off and thought, 'That's a first.'

Duff took a huge chance in taking me from Dundee to Hibs in 1997. I know for a fact he had to persuade the Easter Road board that I would be good for the club. They hadn't been impressed with everything they knew and heard about me. However, Duff stuck at it and, of course, I was overjoyed when I signed for Hibs. For a few months, I was in the form of my life. It was around that period that there were calls from some members of the media to get an international call-up.

I was about thirty-four years old at the time and Duff knew how to handle me. He knew I liked a night out with the boys after the game on a Saturday, so we came to a private agreement that I could take a Monday or two off. I was grateful, but I never took advantage of our friendship. I'll give you an example. David Elliot used to pick me to take me through to Edinburgh, but there was a day when I called him to say I wouldn't be going in. I'm being honest here when I say I was knackered. I wasn't lying and I knew I couldn't go through any training routines that day. I was hurting just about everywhere. I think even my eyelashes were throbbing.

I telephoned Duff to relay the news. He wasn't convinced. I could detect it immediately when I heard him bellow down the line, 'Get fuckin' through here right fuckin' now.' I told him I had missed my lift. 'I don't fuckin' care – just get here,' was the response. There was nothing else for it. I dragged my old bones into a taxi and travelled through from Glasgow to Edinburgh. I think it cost me about £100. I duly arrived and went to talk to Duff. 'Go and see the doc,' he barked. I went for a quick check-up and he found that I was, in fact, knackered. I don't think that was the medical term, but it was agreed that training was definitely out that day. Duff accepted the doc's word and I was told to rest. It cost me one hundred quid to discover I was shattered.

Duff has been brilliant for me. I love his man-management style. He has a no-nonsense attitude and gets the best out of players. He hasn't had the best of luck in the game. I know he loved it at Chelsea, but he was on his way out when Gianluca Vialli was sacked. Then he teamed up with Graham Rix at Portsmouth and that finished the same way when Rixy was fired. At the time of writing, he is at Brechin City and, no disrespect to anyone at the Angus outfit, he deserves to be performing at a much higher level. Maybe it will come because he is still young in managerial terms. I will always remember Duff on STV one day when he was the match analyst at a Partick Thistle game. He said, 'I have no doubts that Chic Charnley will go to the very top in this game.' Sadly, it was one prediction my old pal didn't quite get right.

Duff is a rarity among the footballing fraternity in that he actually turns up on time for everything. There's the old joke from Ally McCoist, a notoriously bad timekeeper. After he had kept a journalist hanging around for about an hour, he eventually turned up, looked at his watch and quipped, 'This is the earliest I have ever been late.' Duff, though, was the exact opposite. If he said he would be somewhere at one o'clock you could bet that's precisely where he would be.

However, I was worried one day when he was running late. I couldn't get in touch with him and it was a very important occasion. Sadly, Jackie McNamara Senior's lovely wife Linda had passed away and we had made arrangements to travel through to Edinburgh together for the extremely sad occasion of her funeral. I talked a lot to Linda on the phone when I had possibly partaken of too much ale. Or pissed, if you prefer. I would make calls to Jackie at all times of the night for a blether and I would end up having a natter with Linda who was blessed with the patience of a saint.

As you would expect, I realised it must be something crucial for Duff to be running late. Eventually, he turned up and told me he had popped in to see his mother-in-law in Maryhill on his way to my home. He parked his car outside the close, spent a half-hour or so chatting away and informed her where he was going that afternoon. To his horror, someone had broken into his car in the short period of time he had spent upstairs. Making matters even worse, his mobile phone had been nicked.

Duff was raging. He went back to his mother-in-law's to use her phone. He dialled his mobile number, and as brazen as anything, a voice answered. Duff reckoned the lad was about ten years old. He said, 'You've got my mobile. I want it back. Now. OK?' The wee ned replied, 'Naw.'

'Look, I'll give you £50 in cash right now if you return it.' Once again, 'Naw' was the reply. Duff blew a gasket. 'You little arsehole. I need that mobile. Give it back or you'll be in big bother.' The ned wasn't impressed by the threat from my pal and replied, 'I'm an arsehole? You're the arsehole who left your fuckin' mobile in your car!' Duff never did get that phone back.

12

SILENCE OF THE LAMBIE?
NO CHANCE!

John Lambie was holding court at the end of a game and he was far from satisfied with what he had just witnessed from his Partick Thistle players. He was letting rip as only he could. I believe he once registered on the Richter Scale and it would be fair to say the F-word was in overdrive. He was going round everyone of us and tearing our performances apart. Then he came to Declan Roche, a young player he had signed from Celtic. He pointed at him and astonished us all by suddenly pulling out a pigeon from somewhere inside his coat. He fixed Declan with a stare that would terrify the devil and said, 'See you, you Irish bastard, you're as useful as this doo.' He then wrung its neck and threw it at the player. Declan just about passed out! It could only happen at Firhill.

Just to put any pigeon fancier's mind at rest, it should be pointed out that the doo hadn't been taking its feed and was dying, anyway. It was the kindest thing to put it out of its misery although God only knows why our gaffer had it with him that day in the first place. Life around John Lambie was never dull, I can assure you of that.

I owe that guy so much but don't believe that just because he signed me a few times that there was any favouritism. Far from it. John Lambie fined me more often than any other manager I ever played with. If he wasn't happy with me, he was never slow to tell me in that inimitable fashion of his. He knew I liked a pint with my old mates from Possil, but he also realised I was a good trainer. I would never have lasted until I was thirty-nine in senior football if I hadn't been. I have heard the tales that I used to walk around with my hands in my pockets as the other guys went through all sorts of routines. Believe me, that is utter and total rubbish. I was at my happiest when we were doing ball work or, and this will surprise you, long-distance running. I've always had a good engine, thankfully, and jogging for miles was never a problem.

Stories about John are the stuff of legend, of course. I recall a time when he took Thistle down to Blackpool as we prepared for a big game. Surely it was just a coincidence that there was a pigeon convention on at the time and, as everyone knew, John was a massive fan of the sport. One night, though, our gaffer must have had something to celebrate because he returned to the hotel more than just a little tipsy. Truth be told, he was pissed.

He started to have a go at some of the players, but one of our lads, Callum Milne, was having none of our manager's rantings. He stopped the boss in mid-flow with a right hook that just about knocked out John. Unsteadily, our boss got back to his feet and made his way to his room. We waited for our gaffer's reaction the following day as we assembled for breakfast. There was silence as he entered the dining room and looked over at Callum. We were amazed to hear him say, 'Good shot, son!' That was the end of the matter.

There was another occasion at Blackpool when things went badly wrong and left our manager heading for the local hospital. The players thought it would be a good idea to throw the boss into the sea after a training session on the beach. Unfortunately, they chucked him in at a shallow point and John punctured a lung when he hit the surface. He wasn't best pleased, I can tell you that. As he scrambled to his feet he growled, 'As soon as I get better I am going to free all you bastards!'

There was a day when we were preparing for training at Firhill and this young lad was introduced to the players. I was far from impressed. He appeared to be festooned in all sorts of Rangers items, shirt, socks and even a ring. I said, 'Come with me.' I marched him to the gaffer's office for a laugh. John Lambie was as big a Rangers fan as I was a Celtic supporter and I opened the door and presented the young lad. 'Look at this, boss,' I said. 'He's supposed to be trying to become a Partick Thistle player and he's got all this Rangers stuff. What do you think?' Lambie didn't even look up. 'Make him captain,' he said.

I remember a time at Thistle when he could have dumped me and I wouldn't have blamed him one bit. I had missed training for about three days before the boss turned up at my front door. Frankly, I had no excuse. I had gone AWOL with some pals on the bevvy. He was grim-faced as he looked at me and said, 'Chic, you know what you have done is totally unacceptable.' He gave me a real dressing down and I felt like a naughty schoolboy being addressed by the headmaster. At the end of it, he simply added, 'The newspapers want me to drop you for your stupidity, but I'm not listening to them. You're playing on Saturday.' I turned up for training on Thursday and put in a pulverising shift. I went through the same routine twenty-four hours later. I knew everything had been my own fault and, as ever, I was quick to put my hands up. I can think of other bosses who'd have been reaching for the P45. I knew I had to repay the gaffer. I scored two goals in the following game on Saturday. I wasn't totally off the hook, though, as I was also fined two weeks' wages. I couldn't argue. To be fair, John Lambie used to talk my kind of language. He was straight and to the point. He didn't shoot round corners and that suited me.

He had a wicked sense of humour, too. I recall him talking to

Justin Fashanu about actress Julie Goodyear, who played the barmaid Bet Lynch in *Coronation Street*. Apparently, they were seen as an item although, as the world knows now, Justin, who had a brief spell at Thistle, was gay and, sadly, committed suicide in a garage in London years later. On this occasion, though, John was chatting to him and enquired, 'That Bet Lynch, Justin – is she any good in the sack?' I can't recall Justin's reply!

Mind you, I wasn't laughing the day the gaffer almost killed me! Young kids used to fire golf balls into Firhill from a mound outside the ground. We could be doing some lapping of the track or suchlike when we would come under a bombardment from these wee rascals. One day I picked up one of the golf balls and, when no-one was looking, I slung it at Lambie. I was bang on target and the ball whacked off the back of his head. He looked round and screamed, 'Who the fuck did that?' I gave him my best innocent look and replied, 'It was one of those wee buggers outside the ground, boss.' He fumed and raged all the way through the rest of the training session and afterwards, when we were in the showers, I decided to tell the truth.

'It was me, boss,' I owned up. 'I'm the culprit. I was just having a wee laugh.' He was remarkably composed given the situation and the fact that, like me, he had a bit of a suspect temperament. I should have smelled a rat. The following day I turned up for training at the usual time. I walked into the dressing room to get changed and the next thing I felt was this awesome weight landing on my head. The gaffer had hidden behind the door and, perched on a chair, he waited for me to make my entrance. Then, with perfect timing, he dropped a medicine ball on my head!

Pain ricocheted through me as I looked round and shouted, 'Gaffer, you could have killed me. You could have broken my neck.' I'll always remember his reply. 'Ach, I only hit you on the head – you're more likely to damage the medicine ball.' I never threw a golf ball at John Lambie again.

There was also the true story of one of our players taking a sore one and being left slightly concussed during a game. The physio ran on to see how the guy was faring. He looked a bit out of sorts, to say the least, and the physio turned to John and said, 'He doesn't know where he is, boss. He doesn't even know who he is.' Quick as a flash the gaffer replied, 'Tell him he's Pele!'

As everyone knows, footballers have some disgusting habits. One day after training at Firhill we went into the dressing room where they had three big communal baths. Look away now if you are faint of heart. Brian Gallagher and I thought it would be good for a laugh to pee in one of the baths. It was intended for one of our team-mates, but to our absolute horror the first guy through the door was John Lambie. Gal and I looked at each other. Which bath would our boss jump into? We were trying to will him away from the one we had peed in. Nope. He went straight for it and leapt in. We both burst out laughing and a puzzled Lambie looked at us. 'What are you two Celtic bastards laughing at?'

Meanwhile, he was throwing the water all over himself, washing his hair and so on. Gal couldn't contain himself any more. He said, 'What do you think of Celtic piss, boss?' Lambie was out of that bath like a shot and, completely naked, chased us down one of the corridors at Firhill. 'I'll kill you Celtic bastards when I get my fuckin' hands on you,' he screamed. Those were the words that echoed around Firhill as Gal and I set a world sprint record.

Actually, I think my old gaffer was pretty much unshockable. During a game against Forfar at Station Park and I was sitting beside him in the dug-out. As usual, he was puffing away merrily on a cigarette. He threw the stub on the ground and I noticed it was still lit. Now I have never smoked in my life, but I picked it up and put it in my mouth. I was having a drag on the discarded cigarette when the boss looked round and said in a matter-of-fact fashion, 'When did you start smoking?' Could you imagine another manager's reaction to one of his players sitting on the touchline smoking a cigarette? I think it would be a fair bet that most would go ballistic. But John Lambie is a complete one-off.

It wasn't often he was rendered speechless, but Billy Connolly managed it one day. Thistle were playing Celtic that day and I was made up that the comedian known to everyone as The Big Yin recognised me and I got my photograph taken with him. He spied John Lambie and said, 'That wee team of yours is doing well, isn't it? Just don't expect anything today, OK?' For once, our boss was tongue-tied. Connolly 1, Lambie 0!

It must be said that the gaffer rescued more than a few footballers and revived a lot of careers that were sailing towards the rocks. My old Clydebank chairman Jack Steedman used to say, 'I see we're playing Thistle at the weekend. That's the usual meeting with a collection of bampots.' And Peter Hetherston, who wasn't a bad midfielder in his playing days with Aberdeen, once remarked, 'Thistle? They're just a gang of thugs in football strips.' Charming.

Jim Oliver was a chairman for whom I had the greatest of respect. I can't say the same for his successor Brown McMaster who, as far as I was concerned, was at Partick Thistle for himself and not the club. That's just the impression he gave me by his overall attitude to the football-playing side of the club. Jim, on the other hand, gave an awful lot of his time to the Jags and cared deeply about every aspect of the club. I'm not too sure if John Lambie took to him at first and he certainly wouldn't have been impressed when our new chairman declared that he knew very little about football. However, as they got to know each other better, they clicked. Jim took care of business matters and

John was allowed to run the football team. And that's the way it should be.

Jim was a member of the exclusive Buchanan Castle Golf Club and one day he invited the playing staff to join him in a day out in the plush surroundings at the club. I'm not a golfer and thought it would be reasonable to be given the day off. Lambie was having none of it. I was told it was a team bonding effort and I had to come along. Jim was a bit wary of me and, naturally enough, had a reputation to protect at this swish club. He told the boss to keep an eye on me. I had to trek around with John, Ronnie Simpson, the former Celtic European Cup-winning goalkeeper who was a coach at the Jags at the time, and a chap called Bobby Law. Boy, was I bored. I knew you had to keep quiet when you were on the course so, as you might expect, I made as much noise as possible.

Lambie hit a shot up against a young tree and I'm told it is golfing etiquette to take a drop shot in this circumstance. Lambie duly picked up his ball and threw it onto the fairway. Ronnie, who was an excellent golfer, said, 'Hey, John, you can only do that if you are up against a young tree. That tree is about 200 years old.' Lambie shot back, 'That's young for a tree!' Ronnie was speechless.

While we are at Hamilton Accies together we had that loud-mouth fan called Fergie who, I'm sure, could be heard on several different continents on matchday. He was a one-man wall of noise and you didn't need other supporters adding to his vocal contribution when he was in full flow. Lambie actually liked this bloke and used to get him tickets for games. There was one day we were coming back from a match in Edinburgh when the boss noticed Fergie on his own. He ordered the driver to stop and let Fergie on the bus. 'Right, no nonsense, Fergie,' said John. 'Keep it zipped.'

You might as well try to stop a charging rhino with a feather.

Fergie just didn't know the meaning of silence being golden. He was on the bus a matter of seconds when he started up. He had a go at our assistant boss Gerry Collins immediately. 'Hey, Collins, you bald bastard,' was his opening gambit. This went for about five minutes until Lambie told the driver to pull over. Even Fergie didn't know what to say when the boss booted him off the coach. 'You had your chance,' he said. 'Now fuck off and make your own way home.'

I remember another incident when Fergie actually had us all in stitches. We were playing Rangers at Ibrox around the time Graeme Souness was hitting the headlines after splitting up with his first wife. Fergie, as usual, used to wait for our coach to arrive outside the stadium. Souness was making his way to the entrance at the same time and Fergie said, 'Good afternoon, Mr Souness.' Everyone knew our celebrated fan and the Rangers boss replied, 'Good afternoon, Fergie.' Before the Rangers gaffer could disappear through the front doors Fergie barked, 'So, Mr Souness, you'll no' be getting your nookie tonight!' I think Fergie might have struck a raw nerve because the Rangers boss played that day and kicked lumps out of every Hamilton player.

We did a photo shoot one day to promote our new strip sponsors at Thistle, Watson Towers. It was a company owned by one of our directors Bobby Watson, the former Rangers player. Lambie took me aside and said, 'Get on to Bobby and see if he'll give you some cash for modelling the gear. You are promoting his firm, after all.' I duly telephoned Bobby and asked if we were due some sort of reward for advertising his company. He thought about it before agreeing to pay for a slap up meal for me and three of my team-mates at a top Italian restaurant in Glasgow. Bobby could have saved himself the money. If he had picked up an early edition of the evening newspaper he would have seen a picture of Lambie, me and Brian Gallagher already on the back page!

John Lambie is nothing if not honest. He tells the story against himself after he had signed Andy Gibson from Aberdeen. The player duly turned up with his agent, the deal was agreed and the lad made his debut the following Saturday. As the game went on, the gaffer's furrowed brow was well in evidence. He shook his head, turned to Gerry Collins and admitted, 'I've signed the wrong fuckin' player – that's not the fuckin' player I wanted.' In fact, the boss had had his eyes on Andy Roddie, who was also at Aberdeen at the time. He got his Andys mixed up. To be fair to Andy Gibson, he did well at Thistle and turned out to be a shrewd buy!

There was another occasion when John, at this time the Hamilton Accies manager, took a shine to a player called Paul Martin who was at Kilmarnock. He was sufficiently impressed by the youngster to put in a £65,000 bid for him – astronomical money for the Douglas Park club. Killie didn't hesitate as they took the cash and Lambie got his player. However, after a couple of games the lad wasn't performing. John wasn't too impressed and shortly afterwards telephoned Eddie Morrison, the Killie boss, and asked him if he wanted Martin back. He said, 'I'll let you have him for £30,000.' Eddie replied, 'No thanks' and put the phone down. Hamilton were stuck with the player.

John was a bit more careful the next time he reached for the club chequebook. Mind you, he has always been careful with his own money!

13

ON THE BOSSES

One of Alex McLeish's first acts as manager of Hibs was to bin me. Fair enough. As I've said in a previous chapter, I don't blame him one bit and I don't hold it against him. So when I say he is one of the luckiest team bosses around please don't think I am having a go at him just for the sake of it. That is most certainly not the case, but I do believe Big Eck has had more than his fair share of good fortune as a manager.

When he took over from Jim Duffy at Easter Road he had plenty of time to stop the club from going into freefall and hurtling towards relegation. He became boss in February with lots of games to play and turn things around. He didn't manage that and I seem to recall he said it was Duff's team that went down. I'm not buying into that. No way. It was Alex McLeish's team that got relegated, let there be no mistake about that.

Duff was sacrificed by the board and his sacking proved once again just how cruel football can be. His last game in charge was a match against Motherwell – managed by Alex McLeish – at Fir Park. At one stage Hibs were leading 2-1 until central defender Brian Welsh was sent off. The roof caved in on us after that and Motherwell went on to win 6-2 with a pile of late goals. A result like that looks horrendous on paper, but, in truth, there were never four goals between the sides until we had Welsh red-carded. McLeish got great praise for bringing Hibs back into the

Premier Division after just a year, but, once again, I think he was lucky. In my book, anyone could have got Hibs promoted after just one year. He was given cash to spend by the board and he was able to bring in the likes of Frank Sauzee and Russell Latapy. They shone in the First Division and the plaudits went to McLeish. I'm not so sure they were entirely deserved.

When he took over from Tommy McLean at Motherwell he inherited a team that was up there challenging at the top with Celtic and Rangers. Wee Tommy had put together a very good team and McLeish just had to point it in the right direction. However, if you examine things a bit more closely and clinically, you will see the part he played in the club's downward spiral. Certainly, the Fir Park support wasn't happy with him and he got it in the neck on more than a few occasions. Hibs offered him an escape route and he was more than happy to take it. And when Rangers came calling I believe Dame Fortune smiled on him once again.

He won all three domestic trophies in his first calendar year at Ibrox, but it was a real hit-or-miss effort that got the Rangers fans onside. They weren't convinced about their new manager at the start and the acid test was the first encounter against Celtic which just happened to be a CIS Cup semi-final at Hampden. I was at Hampden that evening and couldn't believe Celtic weren't about four goals up in the first half-hour. They bossed the game from the start and Henrik Larsson, of all people, passed up a couple of gifts. On one occasion he was clean through on Stefan Klos and, most unlike him, tried to be far too clever. He wanted to stick the ball through the goalkeeper's legs, but his shot was blocked and Rangers escaped. It should have been a goal.

The tie went to extra-time and the gods lavished good fortune on McLeish again when Bert Konterman scored the winning goal. If I ever needed convincing that McLeish was blessed it came with that effort. Konterman wasn't exactly the greatest passer of the ball so when he belted one into the roof of the net from about thirty-five yards with a first-time effort you had to believe that someone up there liked Big Eck. The final in season 2000/01 was between Rangers and First Division Ayr United. The platform was there for McLeish to win his first trophy as Rangers manager. They were odds-on favourites and sauntered to a 4-0 victory. I realise this may come across as someone with a chip on his shoulder, someone who was given his P45 by McLeish, but it is an honest opinion. To blame Duff for Hibs' relegation is ridiculous when you consider McLeish had so many games to turn things around. When things started to go awry at Ibrox he was shifted for Paul le Guen to take over and once more McLeish landed on his feet when he got the Scotland international manager's job.

He received massive kudos for the victory against France in the European Championship qualifiers but we still didn't qualify for the finals. If you put our two wins over the French under the microscope you will see how fortunate Walter Smith and McLeish were. The French scored two perfectly good goals at Hampden that were ruled out for offside when the game was scoreless. Gary Caldwell's second-half winner was more of a tackle than a shot, although, it must be said, I wasn't complaining at the time. And will James McFadden ever score a goal like the one he did in Paris? That shot could have ended up in Marseille, but, as luck would have it, the ball whizzed high past the keeper into the net. I'm not saying it was a fluke – I wouldn't have minded claiming it – but I doubt if we will see another like it. McLeish's stock rose accordingly and it was sufficient for Birmingham City to come in and take him across the border. The luck ran out in his first season down there and, of course, the Midlands outfit were relegated although they were promoted a year later. If Jim Duffy had enjoyed the same sort of fortune as Alex McLeish I have absolutely no doubt he would be managing in the top-flight. And making a success of it, too.

What a double-act! This is my granny Agnes with my son Gary.

Can you spot me? I'm kneeling on the left of the front row with my St Theresa's team-mates (back row, left to right): Joe Sutherland, Michael Jefferies and Joe Hayburn; (front) Me, Stephen Finnan and Frank Redmond.

Happiness is ... our wedding day. My ma Isa is sitting on the right, my da John behind her. Margaret's mum Margaret Kelly is seated on the left with her husband Joe. My young sister, also called Margaret, is extreme left with bridesmaid Jacqueline, another sister, and my brother Edward, the best man, making up the group.

The Cup that cheers! Here I am with my Possil Villa pals (left to right): Podgie Lyttle, Jas Carbon, John Hynd and James McNamara.

Saints alive! Here I am with St Mirren boss Davie Hay and David Elliott after signing for the Paisley side. I wonder what happened to Davie's beard!

On the run! Racing away from Raith Rovers defender Jimmy Nicholl.

Flashpoint! Raith's Jimmy Nicholl is on the ground while I exchange pleasantries with John McStay. St Mirren team-mate John Hewitt tries to intervene.